Bilenski

# Listen Up! SCIENCE

## Activities to Improve Science and Listening Skills

by Ann Richmond Fisher
and Bryce Adam Fisher

illustrated by Bron Smith

Teaching & Learning Company
1204 Buchanan St., P.O. Box 10
Carthage, IL 62321

Cover by Bron Smith



ISBN No. 1-57310-021-8

Printing No. 98765432

**Teaching & Learning Company**
**1204 Buchanan St., P.O. Box 10**
**Carthage, IL  62321**

**This book belongs to**

______________________________

# Dedication

This book is lovingly dedicated
to my parents and Bryce's grandparents,
Russell and Esther Richmond.

# Table of Contents

## Dear Teacher,

You are holding a very unique and useful book—one that combines listening skills with important science information. While your students are learning to listen and follow directions, they will also be learning some significant science material, including phases of the moon, parts of a flower and the functions of different parts of the brain. While some of this may seem a bit sophisticated for the primary grades, students will be able to learn much of this information because they are *listening*, not reading it for themselves. Students (and adults) have a much larger listening vocabulary than reading vocabulary, so students can successfully be exposed to more information, *if* they are good listeners.

This book is designed to be easy for you, the busy classroom teacher, to use. It contains everything from pretests to an answer key. The lessons were also written to be easy to administer. For many of the lessons, your students will need only a piece of paper and pencil. For others they may need crayons or a reproducible page. Materials needed are always listed in the top corner of the page. An answer key is provided in the back of the book which will often help you check students' work with a glance. (It should be noted that in some cases students' answers can vary slightly from the answer key and still be acceptable.)

The science lessons are arranged by topic as listed in the table of contents. Generally, easier lessons are placed first in each section. The content covered is also listed in the top corner of each lesson for your quick reference. It is suggested that you begin with easier lessons that contain information with which your students are already comfortable so that the focus at first will be on *listening*. You may also want to repeat directions two or three times in the beginning and then gradually move towards both harder lessons and less teacher help.

The section that follows, "How to Use This Book," contains more specific instructions on using special features of the book such as the Pre/Posttests and Warm-Ups. It is our goal to help you improve both the listening and science skills of your primary students in an easy, enjoyable manner!

Sincerely,

Ann Bryce

Ann Richmond Fisher and Bryce Adam Fisher

# How to Use This Book

To get maximum benefit from the various features of this book, use the suggestions that follow.

**Warm-Ups:** These are fun activities at the beginning of each section that will introduce students to the upcoming content area. The purpose of the warm-ups is not only to give students a sample of the work ahead but also to get students excited about it.

**Pre/Posttests:** These have been written to help the teacher evaluate student progress. The teacher should carefully preview the upcoming unit before administering the pretest. If some lessons are inappropriate for your class (i.e. too difficult or too easy), then there may also be inappropriate items on the pre/posttest. Feel free to use only the questions on the tests that correspond to lessons in the unit you will actually be using. Come up with your own number for the highest possible test score. Use the **Teacher Record Page** to record the date of each pretest, the number of items on the test and each student's score. After the class completes all appropriate lessons in the unit, administer the same test again, and record student scores for the posttest on the record page. At a glance you can see which students are making significant progress in their listening and science skills. If some students are not improving, try to work with them individually or in small groups to diagnose any problems they may be having.

**Lessons:** Most lessons are written so that you can read them to an entire class while each student completes one page of work. You can then collect the work and evaluate it using the **Answer Key** in the back of the book. Or students can check their own work as the entire class works through the correct solution together. IMPORTANT: In each lesson students are instructed where to write their names on the paper. Make sure they wait and listen to these instructions. Also note that for some lessons such as "Careless Carl" (page 40) and "Tree Time" (page 58), students' answers can vary slightly and still be correct. Students may come up with a different number of answers or have variations in their drawings.

Although the lessons can be administered in a traditional manner described above, some can also be adapted to other formats. A few ideas are listed below. Feel free to use your imagination and try other ideas of your own.

**Small Group Skits:** In "Careless Carl" (page 40) pairs of students could act out different unsafe actions from the story. The rest of the class could guess which part of the story. After listening to the information in "Healthy Work" (pages 42-43) students could act out one of the careers and the rest of the class could try to guess the correct one.

**Chalkboard Lessons:** "Higher or Lower?" (page 10), "Space Sketch" (page 15), "Space Scramble" (page 22) and many others written on plain paper can be done at the chalkboard. You may wish to have three or four students at the chalkboard while the rest work at their seats. This allows you to spot problems immediately and see how you need to pace the instructions. The chalkboard workers may be distracting to the others; students will need to listen and concentrate even harder. They may need to be reminded that other answers may be possible or that other answers may be incorrect. Emphasize the need for each child to do his own best work.

**Team Relays:** Some activities could be done at the board by teams of four to six students working in a relay fashion. "Which Season?" (page 7), "Skyview" (page 22), "What's Not Right?" (page 29) and others could be done in this manner. One member from each team would go to the chalkboard and answer one item, the next member would do the next item, etc. Along the way, other team members would need to be sure they agreed on the correct answer. One person from each team could be given the opportunity to correct earlier mistakes.

**Cooperative Learning Groups:** Some of the listening comprehension lessons and some of the more difficult lessons such as "The First Space Traveler" (page 18), "Moon Mix-Up" (page 24), "Vitamins!" (page 48) and both lessons about dingoes (pages 72-73) can be done in small groups. This requires students to agree on what they've heard and to work cooperatively on a solution.

# Teacher Record Page

| | | Pretest 1 | Posttest 1 | Pretest 2 | Posttest 2 | Pretest 3 | Posttest 3 | Pretest 4 | Posttest 4 | Pretest 5 | Posttest 5 | Pretest 6 | Posttest 6 |
|---|---|---|---|---|---|---|---|---|---|---|---|---|---|
| | Date | | | | | | | | | | | | |
| Student Name | # possible | | | | | | | | | | | | |
| | | | | | | | | | | | | | |
| | | | | | | | | | | | | | |
| | | | | | | | | | | | | | |
| | | | | | | | | | | | | | |
| | | | | | | | | | | | | | |
| | | | | | | | | | | | | | |
| | | | | | | | | | | | | | |
| | | | | | | | | | | | | | |
| | | | | | | | | | | | | | |
| | | | | | | | | | | | | | |
| | | | | | | | | | | | | | |
| | | | | | | | | | | | | | |
| | | | | | | | | | | | | | |
| | | | | | | | | | | | | | |
| | | | | | | | | | | | | | |
| | | | | | | | | | | | | | |
| | | | | | | | | | | | | | |
| | | | | | | | | | | | | | |
| | | | | | | | | | | | | | |
| | | | | | | | | | | | | | |

# Seasons and Weather

**Materials:**
*Reproducible on page 2*
*Pencil*

1. Write your name in the top left corner of the page.
2. In row A, circle the picture that shows how the oak tree would look in spring.
3. In row B, find the clothes you would wear outside to play in the snow. Underline them.
4. In row C, finish drawing the rainbow so it has seven stripes.
5. Write a *P* for purple in the first stripe at the bottom of the rainbow. Write a *Y* for yellow in the fifth stripe from the bottom.
6. In row D, circle the season that tells when Christmas occurs. In row D, underline the season that tells when new leaves form on the bare branches of trees.
7. In row E, underline the cumulus clouds. Cumulus clouds are low, fluffy, puffy white clouds that appear on hot sunny days.
8. In the space marked F on your paper, write your answer to this question: Which of these two cities has the lower average temperature for April? In Tucson, the temperature averages 65°F (18.3°C), and in Mobile, the temperature averages 68°F (20°C). Which is lower? Write *T* for Tucson or *M* for Mobile.
9. In the space marked G on your paper, write your answer to this question: Which of these two cities has the higher average temperature for April? In Minneapolis, the average is 46°F (7.7°C); in Seattle, the average is 49°F (9.4°C). Which is higher? Write *M* for Minneapolis or *S* for Seattle.
10. In row H, circle the word that fits this definition: a long period of dry weather when no rain falls.
11. In row H, underline the word that answers this question: What are the giant electrical flashes that we see in the sky during thunderstorms?

# Seasons and Weather

A.   

B.     

C. 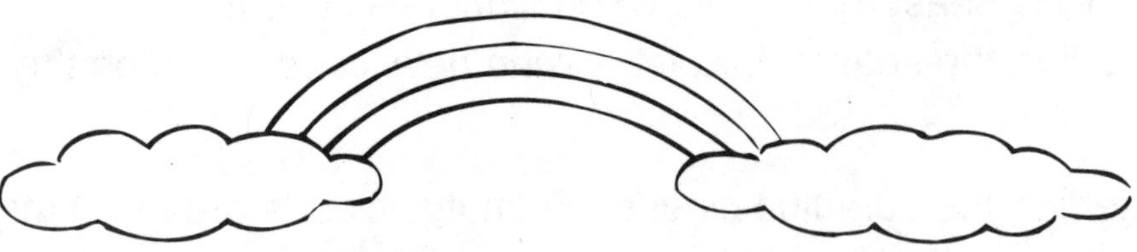

D. spring summer fall winter

E.  

F. ________ G. ________

H. fog drought flood hailstones lightning

**Skills:**
*Identifying differences between spring and fall*
*Drawing*
*Coloring*

**Materials:**
*Blank paper*
*Pencil*
*Crayons*

# Seasonal Scenery

Use as a Warm-Up for Part 1.

Turn your paper so that it is wide and short. In the middle of your page, draw a line from the top of your paper so that you have a left-hand side and a right-hand side. At the top of your left side, write the word *spring*. At the top of your right side, write the word *fall*. Write your name on the back of your paper. Now draw a picture on each half of your paper, following the directions I will give you.

In the spring picture, draw a tree. Be sure it has lots of green leaves for spring. Now draw a matching tree in your fall picture, but show how it would look in the fall. Use your crayons to color the tree.

In the spring picture, draw a garden plot that's ready to be planted with new seeds and plants. In the garden also draw some small, brand-new pumpkin plants. In the fall picture, draw the pumpkin plants again, showing how they would look in fall. Add other full-grown plants to your garden.

In the spring picture, draw some clouds and raindrops.
In the fall picture, draw the sun and a few clouds.

In the spring picture, draw some butterflies.
In the fall picture, draw some geese flying in the sky.

Add a few other features of your choice to both pictures, and finish coloring your page.

**Skills:**
*Choosing appropriate clothing*

**Materials:**
*Reproducible on page 5*
*Crayons: green, yellow, blue, red*

# Dressing for the Weather

I am going to read several directions about what you are to color or write on this worksheet. Some of the items you will use more than once. Be sure to find *all* the answers for each direction.

1. Write your name in the top right corner of your worksheet.
2. Find all the things you would wear if you were going outside to play in the snow. Color all of these things green.
3. Find an item you could use for *two* purposes: to help keep you dry if you were out in the rain and to keep the hot sun off if your were at the beach. Color this item yellow.
4. Find all the items you would need if you were taking a walk in the rain. Circle them with your blue crayon.
5. Find what you would wear if you were going to be outside, and it was just a little cool. Color it with your red crayon.
6. Find what you would wear to go swimming. Color these with your yellow crayon.
7. Finally, find what you would wear to play outside on the playground in the summer. Put a green *X* on these items.

# Dressing for the Weather

Reproducible for use with page 4.

**Skills:**
*Colors of the spectrum*
*Ordinal numbers: 1st to 7th*

**Materials:**
*Blank paper*
*Pencil*
*Crayons: red, blue, green, yellow, purple, orange, blue-violet*

# The Colors of the Rainbow

Let's pretend that you're standing outside on a summer evening with your back to the sun. You're holding a garden hose, and you turn it on so it sprays. Looking into the spray, you see a rainbow. We are going to draw and color that rainbow because all rainbows contain the same colors in the same order.

1. First draw a rainbow on your paper that has seven stripes or layers. (On the chalkboard, show students how to do the first one or two if necessary.) Make the stripes wide enough so you can color them.
2. Start your coloring with the bottom stripe. Color this first stripe purple.
3. Color the second stripe from the bottom with your blue-violet crayon.

Now I'm going to skip around, so listen carefully. Always count from the bottom up.

4. Color the fifth stripe from the bottom with your yellow crayon.
5. Color the seventh stripe from the bottom with your red crayon.
6. Color the third stripe from the bottom with your blue crayon.
7. Color the sixth stripe from the bottom with your orange crayon.
8. Color the fourth stripe from the bottom with your green crayon.
9. Write your name under the rainbow.

# Which Season?

**Skills:**
*Identifying holidays and characteristics of seasons*

**Materials:**
*Lined paper*
*Pencil*

(At the beginning of the lesson, write the words *spring, summer, fall* and *winter* on the chalkboard.)

First number your paper from 1 to 15. Write your name by the number 1.
I have written the names of the four seasons on the chalkboard. For each number on your paper, I am going to name a holiday or describe what happens in nature.
Your job is to figure out in which season each event usually occurs.
Write the name of that season by the correct number.

2. snowfall
3. Fourth of July
4. Easter
5. leaves turn colors and fall from trees
6. Christmas
7. new leaves form on the bare branches of trees
8. Halloween
9. lakes warm up so that people can swim outside
10. pumpkins, squash and apples ripen
11. ice forms on ponds and lakes
12. fruit trees blossom and new flowers grow
13. Thanksgiving
14. squirrels find acorns and store them for winter
15. Hanukkah

# Cloud Cover

Look at the different types of clouds on your paper. I will describe them, one at a time. Listen carefully and try to tell which kind I am describing. Then follow the directions I will give you. Please note that the clouds at the top of the page are highest in the sky, and those at the bottom are lowest in the sky.

1. Find the clouds that are called *cumulus* clouds.
   They are low, fluffy, puffy white clouds that can appear on hot sunny days.
   Draw a *C* on these clouds.
2. Next, find the *nimbostratus* clouds.
   They are mid-level clouds that are thick and dark gray.
   Put an *N* on the nimbostratus clouds.
3. Now find the *cirrus* clouds.
   They look like curly, wispy streaks. They form so high up in the sky that they are made of ice crystals. They are usually a sign of bad weather.
   Write your name on the cirrus clouds.
4. Next I'll describe the *altocumulus* clouds.
   They are mid-level clouds that are flat gray and white blobs of clouds. Sometimes they mean a thunderstorm is on its way.
   Put an *A* on the altocumulus clouds.
5. Now find the *cirrostratus* clouds.
   These are high in the sky and look like flat layers of milky-white clouds. They signal rain.
   Underline the cirrostratus clouds.
6. Finally you should be left with only one more choice.
   Be sure they are the *stratus* clouds by listening to this description: Stratus clouds are low level flat layers of dull gray clouds that often bring rain or snow.
   Draw an *S* on the stratus clouds.

If you think you've made a mistake, listen carefully while I repeat all six descriptions. (Repeat 1-6 above.)

7. Now look back at the cloud picture you labelled with a *C*.
   You may remember that these are cumulus clouds and that they appear on hot sunny days. Turn your paper over and draw a scene of a hot summer day.

# Cloud Cover

Reproducible for use with page 8.

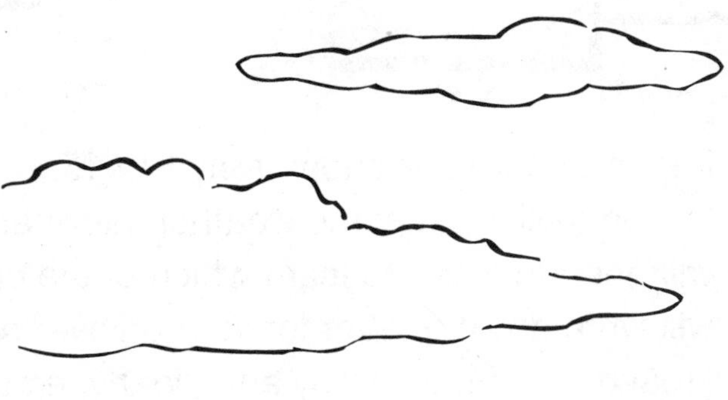

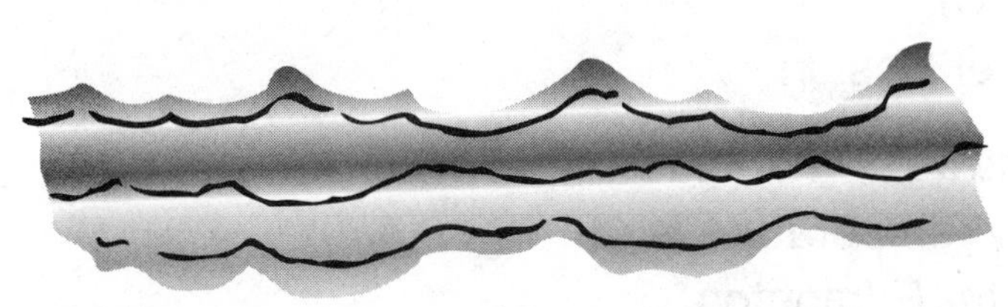

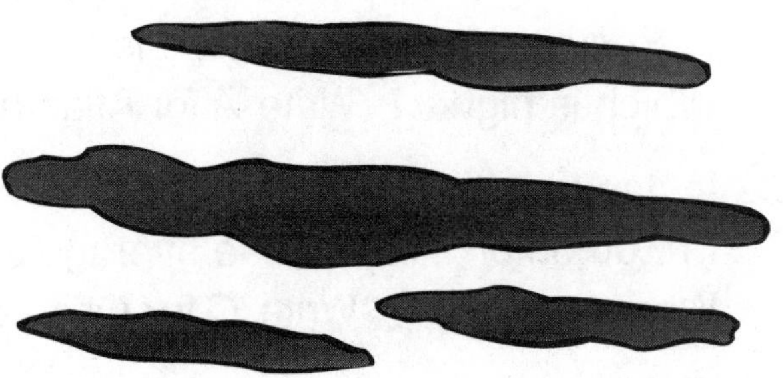

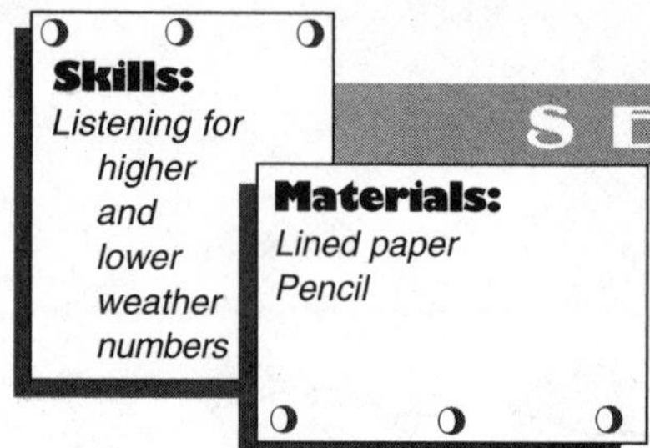




# Higher or Lower?

First number your paper from 1 to 15. Write your name in the top left corner. In this lesson I will read some weather information about different cities. In the first part, you will need to listen to learn which of the cities has the higher temperature. Then you will write down a letter for your answer next to each number on your paper. (Teacher: Speak slowly and clearly, emphasizing the city and the temperature. Do the first one with the class if desired.)

1. The average temperature during July in Chicago is 73°F (22.7°C).
   The temperature for the same month in Las Vegas is 90°F (32.2°C).
   Which is higher? Write *C* for Chicago or *L* for Las Vegas.
2. The average temperature in October for Atlanta, Georgia, is 62°F (16.6°C).
   In Boston, Massachusetts, it is 55°F (12.7°C).
   Which is higher? Write *A* for Atlanta or *B* for Boston.
3. In January, the average temperature in Ottawa, Ontario, is 14°F (-10°C).
   In Edmonton, Alberta, the average January temperature is 13°F (-10.5°C).
   Which is higher? Write *O* for Ottawa or *E* for Edmonton.
4. The average temperature in April in Minneapolis, Minnesota, is 46°F (7.7°C).
   The average temperature during the same month in Seattle, Washington, is 49°F (9.4°C).
   Which is higher? Write *M* for Minneapolis or *S* for Seattle.

Now I will read some more temperatures, but this time I will ask you to listen for the lower temperature.

5. The average temperature during January in Anchorage, Alaska, is 13°F (-10.5°C).
   In Fargo, North Dakota, the average is 4°F (-15.5°C).
   Which is lower? Write *A* for Anchorage or *F* for Fargo.
6. In July, the average temperature in Vancouver, British Columbia, is 64°F (17.7°C).
   The average July temperature in Montreal, Quebec, is 71°F (21.6°C).
   Which is lower? Write *V* for Vancouver or *M* for Montreal.
7. In July, the average temperature in Honolulu, Hawaii, is 80°F (26.6°C).
   In Memphis, Tennessee, the average for the month is 82°F (27.7°C).
   Which is lower? Write *H* for Honolulu or *M* for Memphis.

# Higher or Lower?

8. The average temperature in New York during the month of October is 58°F (14.4°C).
   In Columbus, Ohio, the average is 54°F (12.2°C).
   Which is lower? Write *N* for New York or *C* for Columbus.

Now I will mix up the questions. Sometimes I'll ask for the higher temperature; sometimes I'll ask for the lower temperature.

9. In April, the average temperature in Raleigh, North Carolina, is 59°F (15°C).
   In Providence, Rhode Island, the average is 48°F (8.8°C).
   Which is higher? Write *R* for Raleigh or *P* for Providence.
10. The average temperature in Dallas, Texas, during October is 68°F (20°C).
    In Houston, Texas, the average is 70°F (21.1°C).
    Which is lower? Write *D* for Dallas or *H* for Houston.
11. In July, the average temperature in Washington, D.C., is 79°F (26.1°C).
    In Milwaukee, Wisconsin, the average is 71°F (21.6°C).
    Which is lower? Write *W* for Washington or *M* for Milwaukee.
12. The average temperature during January in Birmingham, Alabama, is 43°F (6.1°C).
    In Tulsa, Oklahoma, the average is 35°F (1.6°C).
    Which is higher? Write *B* for Birmingham or *T* for Tulsa.

For the last three questions, I'm going to ask you which city receives the most or the least rainfall.

13. The city of Quebec receives 33" (88.32 cm) of rainfall a year.
    In Montreal, Quebec, the average rainfall is 31" (78.74 cm).
    Which city receives the least amount of rain? Write *Q* for Quebec or *M* for Montreal.
14. Little Rock, Arkansas, receives an average of 49" (1.24 m) of rain per year.
    Baltimore, Maryland, receives an average of 42" (1.06 m) of rain per year.
    Which city receives the most? Write *L* for Little Rock or *B* for Baltimore.
15. Spokane, Washington, receives an average of 17" (43.18 cm) of rain per year.
    Los Angeles, California, receives an average of 12" (30.48 cm) of rain per year.
    Which city receives the most rainfall? Write *S* for Spokane or *L* for Los Angeles.

(Note: This information came from *The 1994 Information Please Almanac* published by Houghton Mifflin Company. Such reference books contain a wealth of material suitable for adaptation into a variety of listening lessons.)

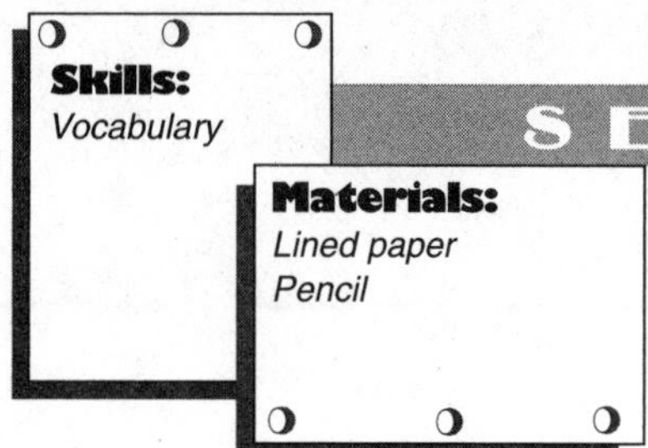




# Weather Words

Write the following words on the board at the beginning of the lesson. Say the words aloud with the class.
(Teacher: Vary the words and definitions according to abilities of class.)

| | | | |
|---|---|---|---|
| air | flood | hailstones | smog |
| dew | fog | lightning | snowflakes |
| drought | frost | rainbow | tornado |

Write your name in the top right corner of your paper. Number your paper from 1 to 12. For each number on your paper, I am going to read the meaning of one of the weather words listed on the board. Listen carefully to each definition or question. Then write the correct word from the list by the number on your paper.

1. What is it that makes up the Earth's atmosphere?
2. What do you sometimes see when the sun comes out after it rains?
3. What do we call moisture that forms at night in small drops on the ground and other surfaces?
4. A long period of dry weather when no rain falls is called a ________.
5. A dangerous funnel-shaped whirlwind that reaches to the ground and destroys objects in its path is called a ________.
6. Pieces of ice that form in clouds (often during thunderstorms) and fall to the ground are called ________.
7. What are giant electrical flashes that we see in the sky during thunderstorms?
8. A cloudy haze of moisture that can prevent us from seeing clearly is called ________.
9. A mixture of smoke and fog is called ________.
10. The opposite of a drought is a ________.
11. What do we call six-sided shapes that form in cold air and fall to the ground?
12. If dew on the ground freezes, it becomes ________.

# Space

**Materials:**
Reproducible on page 14
Pencil

Write your name in the top right corner of your paper.

1. Look at the circle in number 1. This represents the Earth. Write a capital *E* in this circle. Now draw a smaller circle to the right of the Earth. This represents the moon. Write a small *m* above the moon. Draw a dotted line to show the path the moon takes around the Earth. The line should start at the moon, go all the way around the Earth and end at the moon.

2. In row 2 you will see three pictures that tell the history of space flight. You need to put them in order as you listen to my directions. The first space traveler was a dog. Find this picture and put a 1 under it. Next, a man was sent up in a spacecraft. Find this picture and put a 2 under it. The third picture is of a man walking on the moon. Put a 3 under this picture.

3. In row 3 you are going to connect the dots to make a constellation. Connect the dots in order from 1 to 7. Then go back and connect the 4 to the 7. You have drawn the Big Dipper. Shade in the cup part of the dipper with your pencil.

4.-6. For the blanks in 4, 5 and 6, follow these directions. I will tell you the name of an object in space. If it is natural, write the letter *N* in the blank. If it is artificial or man-made, write the letter *A* in the blank. For number 4, the object is a *rocket*. For number 5, the object is a *comet*. For number 6, the object is a *planet*.

7.-8. For numbers 7 and 8, I will read a group of letters. Write these letters on the first blank by each number. Then unscramble the letters to spell a space word. Write the new word in the second blank. The letters for number 7 are *R T S A*. The letters for number 8 are *O N O M*.

9. Now look at the words in row 9. I will read these words to you. If you think the word is the name of a planet, circle it. If you think the word is not a planet, then it is the name of a star and you should put an *X* on it. (Read Saturn, Arcturus, Sirius, Venus.)

10. In row 10 put the moons in order to show the waning phases of the moon–when the moon appears to get smaller. First put a 1 under the full moon, the moon that is completely light. Then put a 2, 3 and 4 under the others in the right order to show the light part of the moon becoming gradually smaller.

# Space

Reproducible for use with page 13.

1. 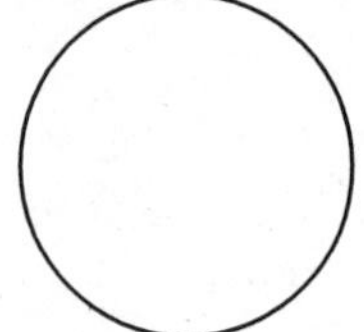

2.   

3. •1 •2 •3 •4 •5 •6 •7

4. ____________ 5. ____________ 6. ____________

7. ____________ ____________ 8. ____________ ____________

9. Saturn Arcturus Sirius Venus

10. 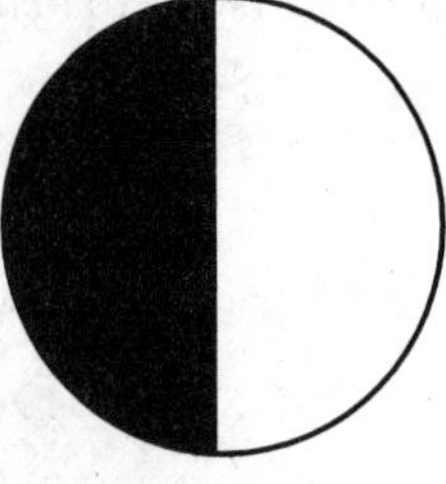 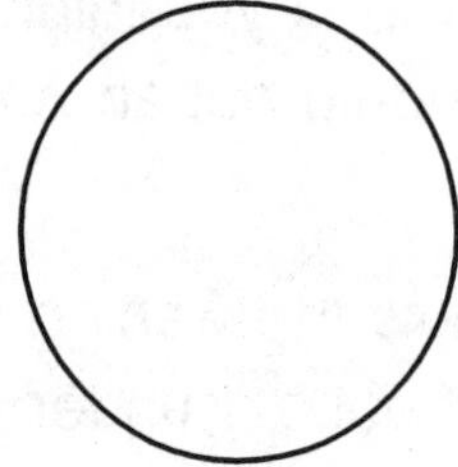

______ ______ ______ ______

**Skills:**
*Relationship of Earth, moon and sun*

**Materials:**
*Just students*

# Space Skit

Use as a Warm-Up for Part 2.

Arrange the class into groups of three students each.

Each of your groups will make a small version of part of our solar system. Decide who in your group will be the sun, who will be the Earth and who will be the moon. (If desired, give the children "clues" to determine these parts such as the child with the darkest [lightest, shortest] hair will be the moon, etc.)

Now have the "sun" stand in the middle of your group. Next, have the "Earth" slowly walk around the sun. Finally, have the "moon" walk around the Earth while the Earth is walking around the sun. Trade parts.

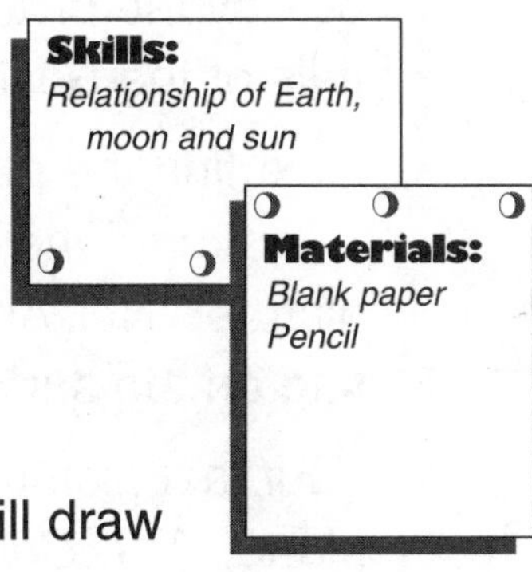

# Space Sketch

(You may wish to use this in addition to or in place of the skit above as a Warm-Up for Part 2.

You are going to draw a picture of part of our solar system. You will draw the Earth, the sun and the moon.

Start by making a large circle in the middle of your page. Write the word *sun*–S U N, inside your circle.

Next, on the left side of the sun draw a medium-sized circle. This will represent the Earth, so put a capital *E* inside this circle. Now draw a dotted line that goes around the sun, stopping and starting at the Earth. This dotted line shows the path the Earth takes as it travels around the sun.

Next, make a very small circle to the left of the Earth. This circle represents the moon. Label it by writing a small *m* above it. Now draw another dotted line to show how the moon travels. This dotted line should go around the Earth, stopping and starting at the moon.

Write your name to the right of the sun.

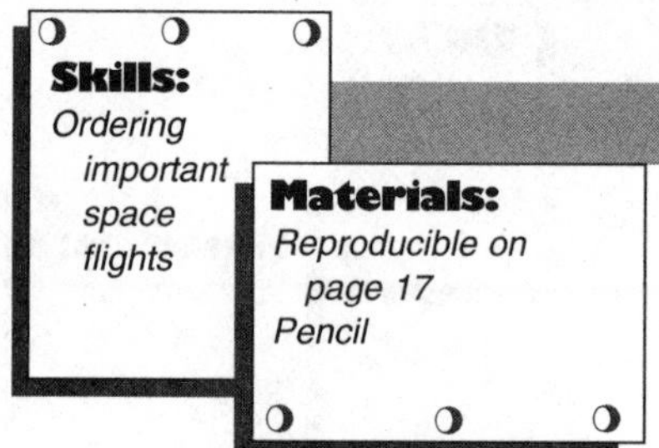




# Space Sequence

Write your name in the top right corner of the page. On this page you will see four pictures that show some important events in space travel. You need to listen so you can put these pictures in order and follow some other directions, too.

1. Find the picture that shows the Earth and a rocket. Put a 1 in the small box by this picture. This reminds us that in 1962 John Glenn became the first American to orbit (or go around) the Earth. This flight lasted less than five hours. Draw a dotted line that shows the path of the rocket around the Earth.
2. The next picture I want you to find shows an astronaut outside of a spaceship. This reminds us of the first time anyone went on a "space walk." The man who did this was Aleksei Leonov from the former Soviet Union. Put a 2 in the small box by the picture. Write the letters *USSR* on the spaceship. These were the initials of the Soviet Union.
3. Next find the picture of an astronaut on the moon. This tells us about Neil Armstrong, the first man to walk on the moon. Put a 3 in the small box by this picture. Neil Armstrong was an American astronaut, and he placed an American flag on the surface of the moon. Draw a flag on the moon in your picture.
4. Your last picture should show a space shuttle. This looks somewhat like an airplane. The *Columbia* was the first space shuttle, and it made its first flight in 1981. Put a 4 in the small box by the space shuttle. The shuttle was the first spacecraft designed to be used over and over. Since *Columbia* there have also been other shuttles. These are American spacecrafts, so write the letters *USA* on the shuttle.

# Space Sequence

Reproducible for use with page 16.

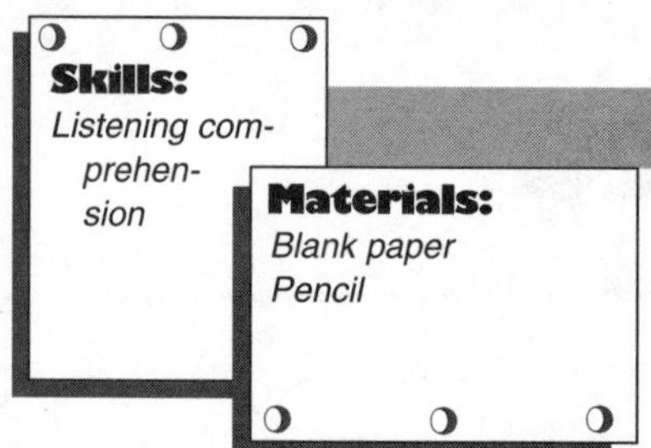


# The First Space Traveler

I am going to read some information about early space travel. When I am done I will ask you to answer some questions, so listen carefully.

In October of 1957, a huge rocket blasted into space from the Soviet Union. *Sputnik 1* was carried in the last section of the rocket. *Sputnik 1* was the first man-made satellite in space. (A satellite is an object that travels around a larger object.) *Sputnik 1* looked like a small shiny aluminum globe. It was only 2 feet (.61 m) across! *Sputnik 1* orbited (traveled around) the Earth and sent radio signals back to stations in the Soviet Union.

About a month later, the Soviet Union sent up their next satellite. It was called *Sputnik 2*. On board *Sputnik 2* was the first space traveler. Who–or what–do you think it was? It was not an astronaut or a scientist or even a human being. The first space traveler was a dog named Laika! Laika made her trip around the Earth inside a tiny cabin. The cabin was attached to the rocket. Laika could get her own food and water from special containers. There were instruments that gathered information about how Laika was getting along.

Sadly, the scientists didn't know how to bring Laika back to Earth, so she died in space. But Laika was an important part of the early space program. Her trip in space taught scientists how people could live in space during future space travels.

# The First Space Traveler

Now number your paper from 1 to 6. Write the answer to each question next to its number.

1. Who was the first space traveler?
   Write *A* for astronaut or *D* for dog.
2. What was this traveler's name?
   Write *L* for Laika or *O* for Orbit.
3. What is a satellite?
   Write *O* for an object that travels around a larger object or *R* for a rocket launched into space.
4. What country sent up the satellites in this story?
   Write *J* for Japan or *S* for Soviet Union.
5. What were the names of the satellites?
   Write *P* for *Pluto 1* and *Pluto 2* or *S* for *Sputnik 1* and *Sputnik 2*.
6. What did scientists learn from the first space traveler?
   Write *U* if they learned more about the planets of the universe or *P* if they learned more about how people could live in space.

Now on the bottom of your page, draw a picture of what the *Sputnik 1* satellite may have looked like. (Remember, it was a small, shiny aluminum globe.)

Write your name under your drawing of *Sputnik 1*.

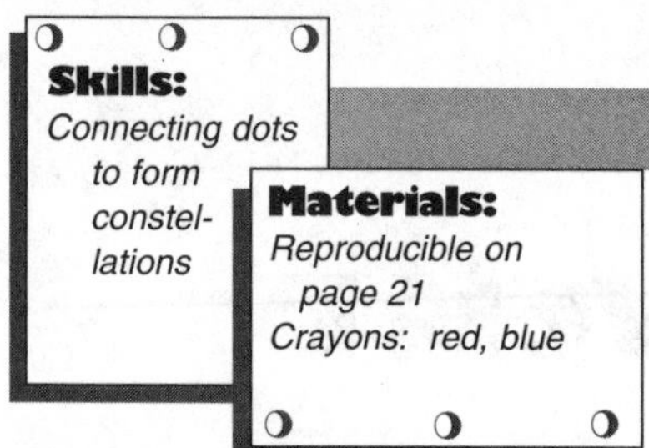




# Star Dots

Groups of stars that form shapes in the sky are called constellations. (Have children repeat the word *constellation*.)

Your paper looks like a page from a dot-to-dot book. Do not connect any dots until I tell you to because this is a special drawing, and we have special instructions.

First take your red crayon. Start at dot 1 and connect these dots in order with straight lines: 1, 2, 3, 4, 5, 6 and 7. Stop at dot 7. Now go back and draw a line to connect dot 4 and dot 7. You have just drawn the Big Dipper. The Big Dipper is a group of seven bright stars that you can see in the sky at night. When we connect these stars, it looks like a dipper with a handle and a bowl.

Now with your blue crayon, start at dot 7 and connect dots 7, 8, 9, 10, 11, 12, 13, 14, 15 and 16. Also connect dot 16 to dot 1. Now go back to dot 8 and connect it to dot 17. Then connect 17 to 18 and 18 to 12. This larger constellation is called the Great Bear. Can you see the bear? Dot 1 is his nose. Dots 10, 11, 12, 13 and 14 are his paws. The Big Dipper is like the bear's saddle.

Write your name under the Great Bear.

# Star Dots

Reproducible for use with page 20.

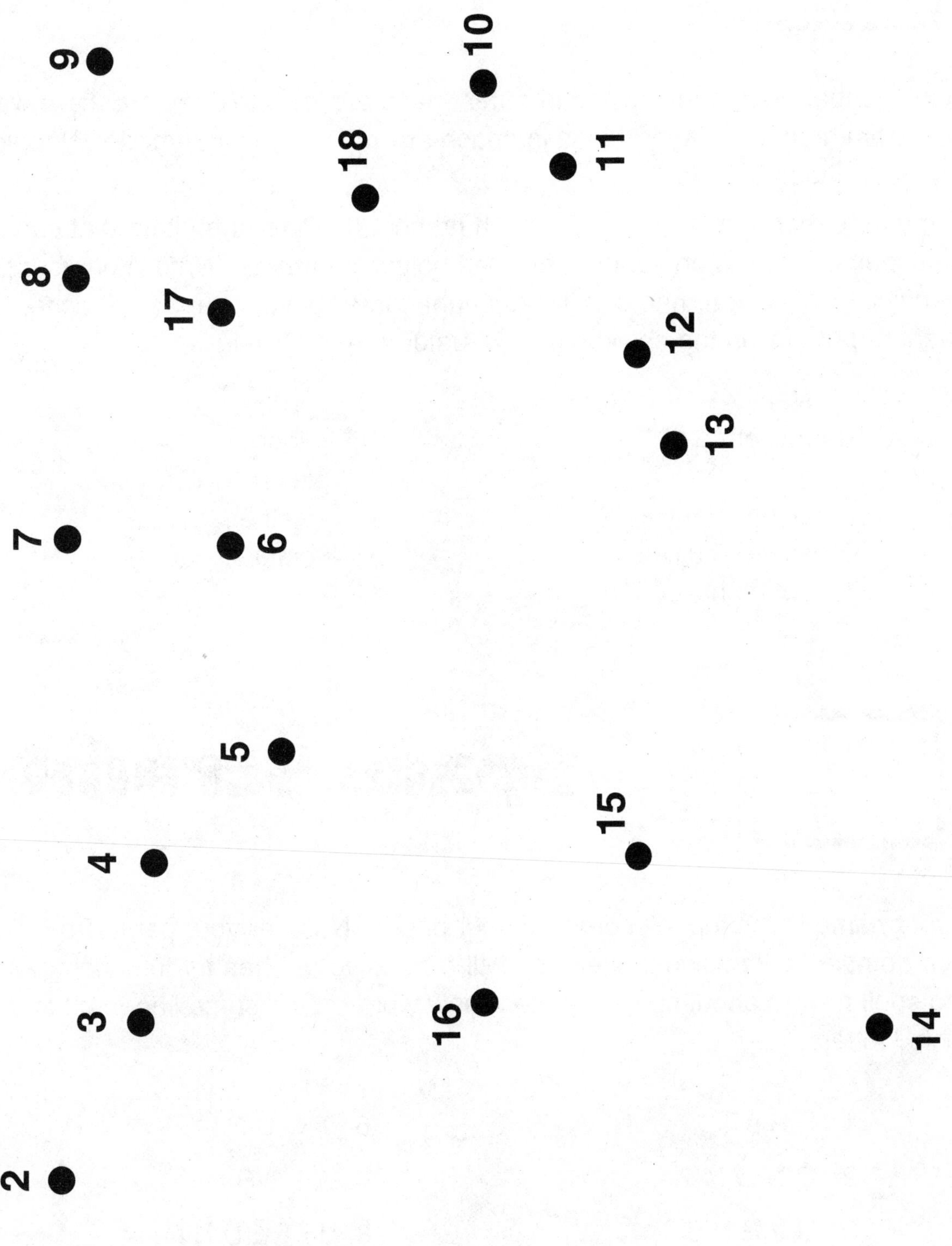

**Skills:**
*Recognizing differences between natural and man-made objects*

**Materials:**
*Lined paper*
*Pencil*

# Skyview

Some things that are in the sky and in outer space are *natural*–they are there without any help from humans. Other things in space are *artificial* or man-made. People, not nature, made these objects.

Number your paper from 1 to 12. For each number, I will read an item that can be found in space. Write *N* on your paper if the object is natural. Write *A* on your paper if it is artificial. Write your name in the top right corner of your paper. (Teacher: You may want to put this on the chalkboard: N–natural, A–artificial.)

1. star
2. rocket
3. moon
4. cloud
5. space shuttle
6. hot air balloon
7. sun
8. rainbow
9. planet
10. weather satellite
11. comet
12. kite

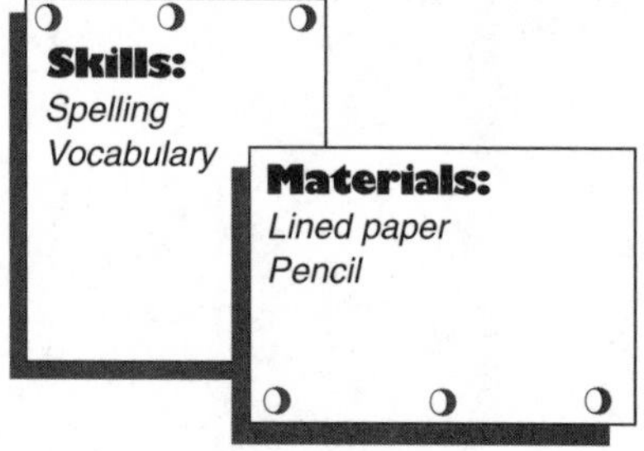


# Space Scramble

Write your name in the top left corner of your paper. Number your paper from 1 to 10. By each number, write down the letters I will read to you. Then try to unscramble them to spell a word about space. Write a new word on the same line, next to the scrambled letters.

1. S R A T
2. O N O M
3. U V E N S
4. N U S
5. A R M S
6. T O U P L
7. A T E R H
8. J I T E U R P
9. T O M E C
10. P I P E D R

**Skills:**
*Recognizing names of planets*

**Materials:**
*Lined paper*
*Pencil*

# Planets and Stars

How well do you know the names of the planets? Let's find out! Number your paper from 1 to 15. I will read a list of words that contains the names of all nine planets plus the names of six stars. For each number, I will say one word. If that word is a planet, write a *P* by the number. If that word is not a planet, it has to be a star, so write *S* by the number.

1. Earth
2. Jupiter
3. Vega
4. Neptune
5. Rigel
6. Mars
7. Venus
8. Mercury
9. Saturn
10. Spica
11. Sirius
12. Pluto
13. Capella
14. Uranus
15. Arcturus

Now double check your work. You should have written the letter *P* nine times and the letter *S* six times. Write your name under your last answer.

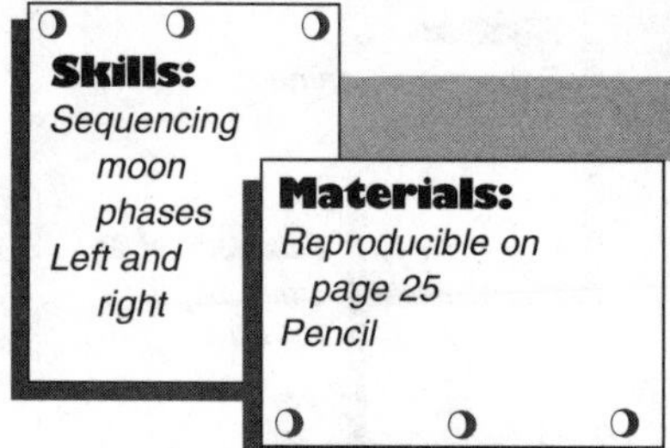




# Moon Mix-Up

The circles on your paper represent the moon. The light portions show the part of the moon that we can see. As you may know, the moon appears to grow larger through part of the month, and then it appears to get smaller again as it moves around the Earth.

I want you to listen to my directions as we put these drawings of moon phases in order. (While there are about 30 phases in all, our page shows just some of them.)

The top left drawing shows a new crescent moon. It is the first one in our sequence. Put a 1 under the top left drawing. Just to the right of that is our second drawing. It is a crescent moon slightly larger than the first. Put a 2 under the second moon in the top row.

The rest of the moons are jumbled up. Next find the first quarter moon. Its left half is black and its right half is light. Put a 3 under this moon. Find the fourth moon where a little more than half of the moon is light and the dark portion is on the left of the moon. Put a 4 under this moon.

Next find the full moon. This is completely light. Put a 5 under the full moon. Also write your name inside the full moon. The first five moons that you have numbered are some of the *waxing* phases of the moon where the moon appears to get larger. Next we'll look at some of the *waning* phases where the moon appears to get smaller.

Our sixth moon will be the one that looks slightly smaller than the full moon in number 5. The small dark portion will be on the right side of the circle. Put a 6 under this moon. The moon that comes next has a slightly smaller light portion than the number 6 moon and a slightly larger dark side on the right. Put a 7 under this moon.

Now find the last quarter moon. It is light on the left half and dark on the right half. Put an 8 under this moon. Now find the moon that has a light crescent on the left side and a dark portion that's slightly larger than the moon numbered 8. Put a 9 under this crescent moon.

Finally you should have just one moon left. It is an old crescent. It should have a very thin light crescent on the left side. Put a 10 under the old crescent moon.

# Moon Mix-Up

Reproducible for use with page 24.

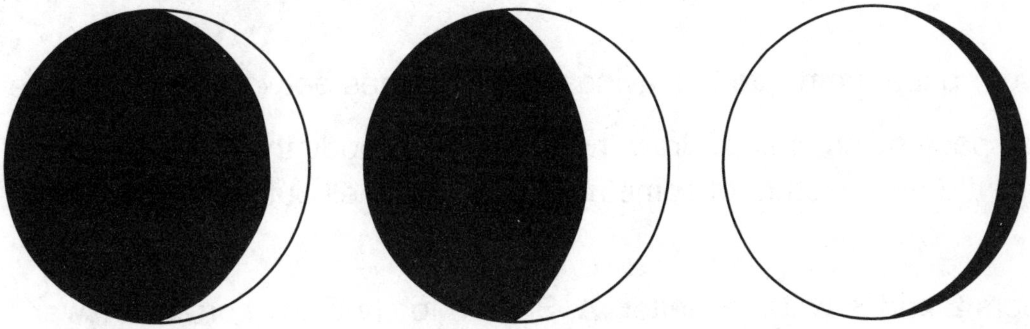

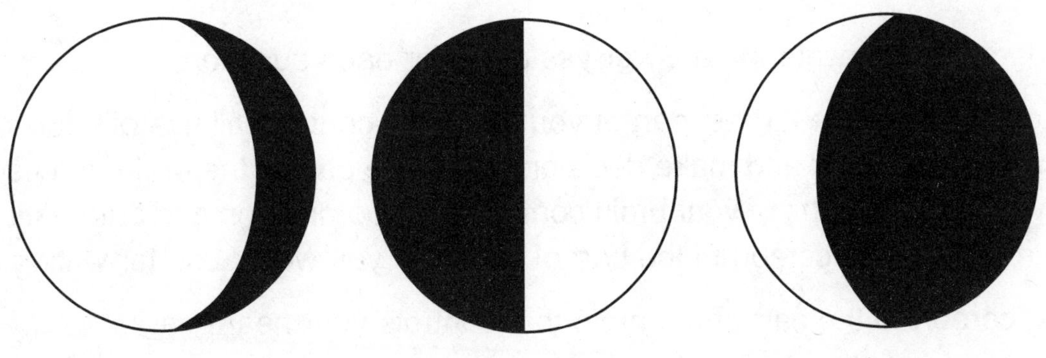

PRE/POSTTEST FOR PART 3

# The Human Body

Number your paper from 1 to 9, leaving two blank lines between each number.

1. In the space by number 1, draw the part of your body that helps you smell. Next to it draw a picture of something you can smell outside.

For numbers 2 and 3, write the letter (A, B or C) to show the correct answer to each question.

2. Which body part does not help you breathe? A. tonsil B. lung C. nose
3. Which body part does not contain a bone? A. hand B. shoulder C. ear
4. In this space, draw a person's arm from the shoulder to the fingers. Put *W* where the wrist belongs. Put an *E* where the elbow belongs.
5. In this space draw the outline of a person's head. Draw in a line showing the lower jaw. This is called the mandible.

For numbers 6 and 7, write the letter for the answer to each question.

6. The longest bone in your body is the femur. Is it in your arm or your leg? Write *A* for arm or *L* for leg.
7. Your ribs are attached to your sternum. Is the sternum in your chest or your back? Write *C* for chest or *B* for back.

For numbers 8 and 9 write the answer *yes* or *no* for each question.

8. The cerebrum is the largest part of your brain. It controls all five of your senses. It is where you think and make decisions. It is the part of the brain you use to read and write. Other parts of your brain control your coordination and automatic jobs like breathing. Is your cerebrum the part of the brain you would use for writing a letter?
9. Is the cerebrum the part of the brain that controls your heartbeat?
10. Write your name at the bottom of your paper.

**Materials:**
*Students*

# Body Action

Use as a Warm-Up for Part 3.

(Teacher: Read this slowly at first and have children act out the motions described. Increase the speed as children become more comfortable with it. Encourage them to say the rhyme with you.)

Nod your head and twist your wrist.
Wrinkle up your nose.
Scratch your back and thump your chest.
Wiggle all your toes.
Bend your elbows; swing your hips.
Blink your lovely eyes.
Pinch your cheeks and touch your chin,
Then pat both your thighs.
Open your mouth; rub your ears.
Bend your bony knees.
Shrug your shoulders; stomp your feet.
Then kindly sit down, please!

by Ann Richmond Fisher

(Another good listening warm-up is the game Simon Says. Give lots of instructions that require the use of different parts of the body.)

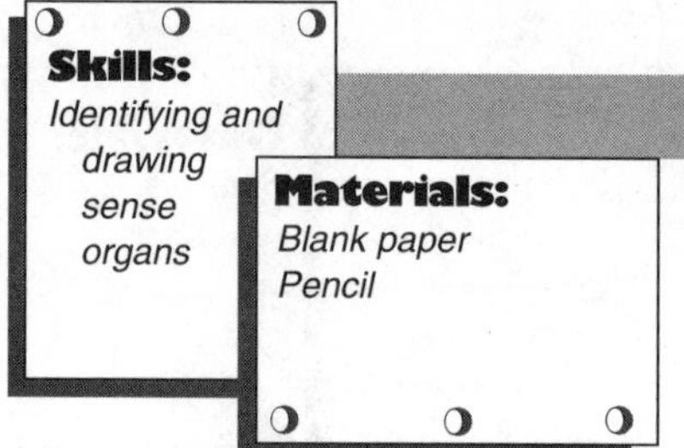




# "Sense"ible Work

1. Fold your paper in half lengthwise.
   Fold it again crosswise so that it is divided into four parts.
2. Unfold your paper and flatten it out. Write your name in the top right corner of your page.
3. In the top left quarter of your paper, draw the part of your body that helps you hear. Also in that box draw something that you hear in your home. (Allow the necessary time for this.)
4. In the bottom left quarter, draw the part of your body that helps you taste. Also draw a picture of something that tastes sweet.
5. In the top right quarter, draw the part of your body that helps you smell. Also draw a picture of something outside that has a pleasant smell.
6. In the bottom right quarter, draw the part of the body that enables you to see. Also draw a picture of something in this room that you can see from your seat.
7. Now turn your paper over. On the back draw a picture of something that would feel sharp. Also draw a picture of someone touching it.

(Teacher: Then write these words on the board: *see, smell, taste, touch, hear.*)

8. Now look at the words I have written on the board. Let's read them together. Write one of these words by each picture that you have drawn. Match the right sense to the right picture.

**Skills:**
*Classifying body parts*

**Materials:**
*Blank paper*
*Pencil*

# What's Not Right?

Write your name in the top left corner of your page. Number your paper from 1 to 10. For each number on your paper I will read a question and three possible answers. One of the answers is not correct. Write the letter of that answer by the number on your paper. (Do the first one together as an example.)

1. Which of these body parts is not in your mouth?
   A. tooth B. tongue C. lung
2. Which of these is not a sense organ?
   A. ear B. heart C. nose
3. Which part does not help you breathe?
   A. tonsil B. lung C. nose
4. Which does not help your blood move?
   A. veins B. heart C. stomach
5. Which does not help you digest your food?
   A. mouth B. lung C. stomach
6. Which body part does not contain a bone?
   A. hand B. shoulder C. ear
7. Which body part does not help you to move?
   A. stomach B. bone C. muscle
8. Which body part is not in your chest?
   A. rib cage B. kneecap C. heart
9. Which body part is not below the waist?
   A. throat B. ankle C. hip
10. Which body part is not part of the head?
    A. brain B. eye C. elbow

(This activity can be made more difficult for older students by adding a fourth choice and/or by altering the questions.)

**Skills:**
*Identifying parts of the body*

**Materials:**
*Reproducible on page 31*
*Pencil*

# Body Parts

For this lesson you will need to find different parts of the human body on the body on your worksheet. Listen carefully and follow the directions.

1. Write your name on the **chest** of the body.
2. Find the **waist** on this body. Draw a belt around the waist.
3. Draw 2 **eyes** in the correct places.
4. Find the **elbows**. Write the letter *E* where each elbow belongs.
5. Find the **wrists**. Draw a bracelet on each wrist.
6. Find the **knees**. Draw a circle where each knee belongs.
7. Find both **ankles**. Write the letter *A* on each ankle.
8. Put the letter *N* where the **nose** should be.
9. Find the **shoulders**. Write the letter *S* on each shoulder.
10. Add 2 **ears** in the right locations.
11. Find the **hips**. Write the letter *H* where each hip belongs.
12. Find the **feet.** Write the letter *F* on each foot.
13. Circle both of the **hands** on this body.
14. Finally, put a **mouth** on this body.

# Body

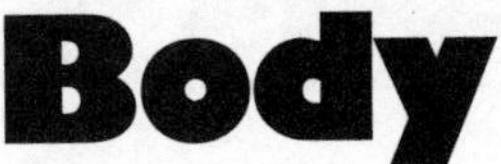

Reproducible for use with pages 30 and 32.

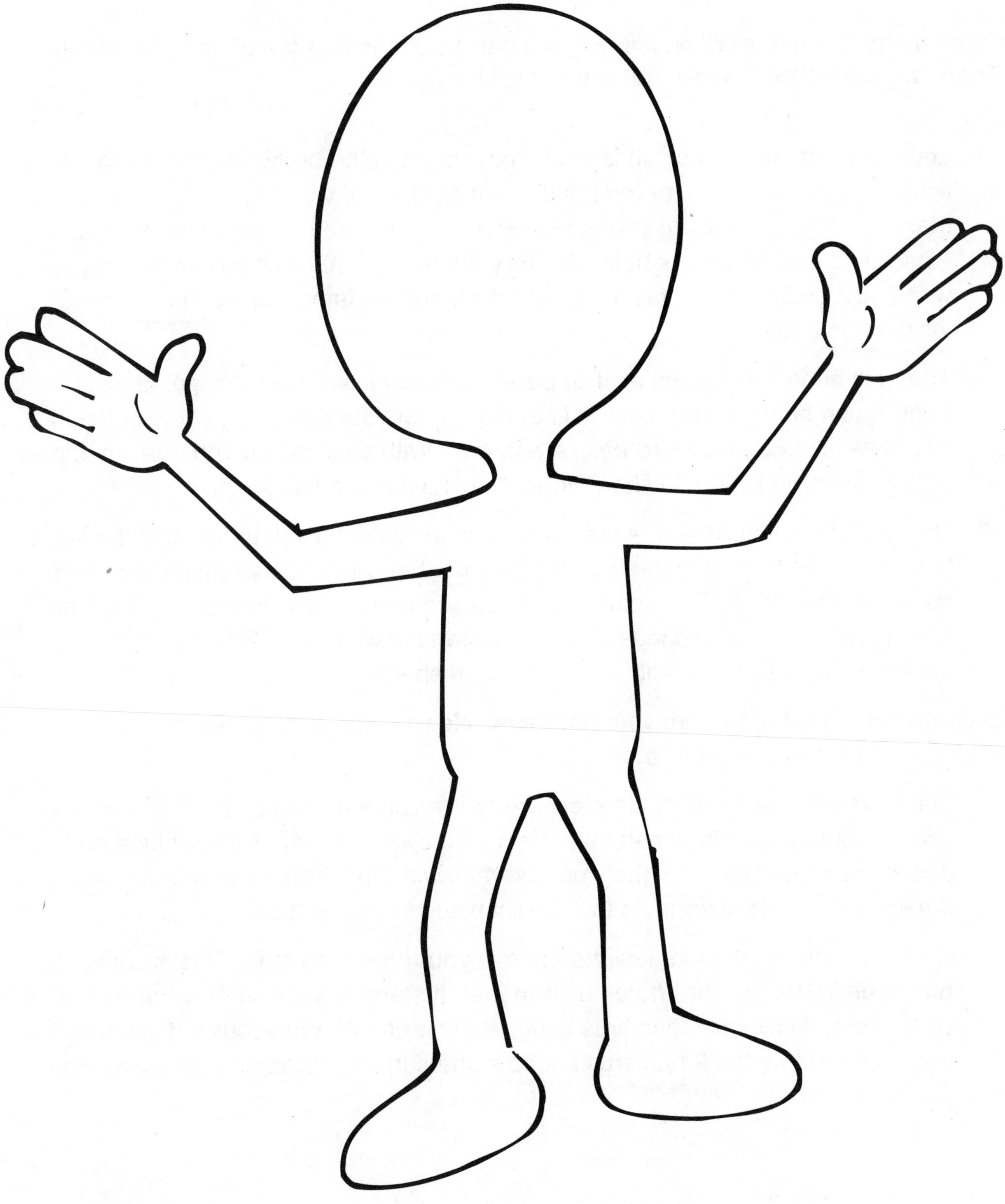

# Bone Zone

Today we're going to work on learning the names of some of the bones in the body. There are more than 200–we will learn only six.

1. Let's start with the **femur**. It is the longest bone in the body. Where do you think it is? It's the thighbone, or the bone in the top part of your leg. It is a long bone that goes from your hip to your knee. Put your left hand on your left femur and your right hand on your right femur. Say the word *femur* with me. Now on your worksheet using a blue crayon, draw in lines for the femur bones in the correct location on each leg.
2. The next bone is the **patella**. The patella is also called the kneecap. It's the front, round bone on your kee. It is at the end of your femur. Feel each of your own patellas. Say the word *patella* with me. With your red crayon, draw two circles on your worksheet to show where the patellas are located.
3. Now we'll find your **tibias**. A tibia is sometimes called a shinbone. It is the larger bone in the lower part of the leg. It's the one that doesn't have much "padding," so it gets bruised easily. It starts at the patella and ends at the ankle. Find the tibia in each of your own legs. Say the word *tibia* with me. With your green crayon, draw the lines for two tibias on your worksheet.

Let's review. Show me where your patella is. Now touch your left femur. Finally, show me your right tibia.

4. The next bone we'll find is the **sternum** or breastbone. It is in the center of your chest. Your ribs are attached to it. Feel your own sternum. Notice that it ends above your stomach. Say the word *sternum* with me. With your yellow crayon, draw a line for the sternum in the correct place in your picture.
5. Next with your right hand, feel the bone in your upper left arm. This is called the **humerus**. Say the word *humerus* with me. It starts at your shoulder and ends at your elbow. How many humerus bones do you have? With your red crayon, draw the lines for the 2 humerus bones in the correct places on your worksheet.

# Bone Zone

**Skills:**
*Identifying bones*

**Materials:**
*Reproducible on page 31*
*Crayons: blue, red, green, yellow*

6. Let's learn one more bone. Your head, or skull, contains many bones, but onlyone of them moves. Can you guess which one it is? It is the lower jaw or **mandible**. Say the word *mandible* with me. Feel your own mandible as you open and close your mouth. On your worksheet with your yellow crayon, draw a bone in the lower jaw shaped like your own mandible.
7. Write your name next to the head on your worksheet.

Optional Review Activity:

On the back of your paper, number from 1 to 6. Write the letter of the answer for each question I will read you.

1. The longest bone in your body is the femur. Is it in your arm or leg? Write *A* for arm or *L* for leg.
2. The mandible is the only movable bone in your skull or head. Is it the upper jaw or lower jaw? Write *U* for upper or *L* for lower.
3. What was the name for your kneecap? Write *P* for patella or *S* for sternum.
4. What bone in your leg is also known as the shinbone? Is it the tibia or the humerus? Write *T* for tibia or *H* for humerus.
5. Your ribs are attached to your sternum. Is the sternum in your chest or back? Write *C* for chest or *B* for back.
6. Is the humerus bone in your arm or hip? Write *A* for arm or *H* for hip.

**Skills:**
*Understanding of the brain*
*Listening comprehension*

**Materials:**
*Reproducible on page 36*

# Brain Bender

First write your name in the top left corner of your page.

Your worksheet shows what the three main parts of the brain look like. Each part looks different and has a different job. In this lesson you will learn about those jobs. I will give you some instructions to follow while I'm explaining the jobs of the brain to you. When I'm done, I will ask you some questions, so please listen carefully.

The largest part of the brain is called the cerebrum. Put a number 1 on the cerebrum. Different areas of the cerebrum enable you to do different things. For example, the back portion near the bottom (this is on your left) is the part of the brain that makes it possible for you to see. Other areas of the cerebrum control your ability to hear, talk, taste, read, write and so on. The cerebrum controls all five of your senses. Certain parts of your cerebrum make the muscles of your body move. Your cerebrum is where your thoughts are formed. Write the letters *S*, *T* and *M* in the cerebrum. These letters stand for the words *senses, thoughts* and *movement*, which are some of the jobs of the cerebrum.

Another part of your brain is called the cerebellum. On your worksheet, it is the small part of the brain on the left side under the cerebrum. It has horizontal lines drawn in it. Put a number 2 on the cerebellum. The cerebellum controls your balance and coordination. It helps you coordinate your arms and legs when you swim or turn cartwheels. It also helps you not to fall when you walk and run. Write *C* on the cerebellum. *C* stands for coordination.

The third part of your brain is called the brain stem. In your drawing, it is the small part coming down under the cerebrum. It has no lines in it. Put a number 3 on the brain stem. The brain stem has nerves that control your breathing, the beating of your heart, the way you digest food and other things your body does automatically–without you thinking about them. Put the letter *A* on the brain stem. This *A* stands for automatic.

# Brain Bender

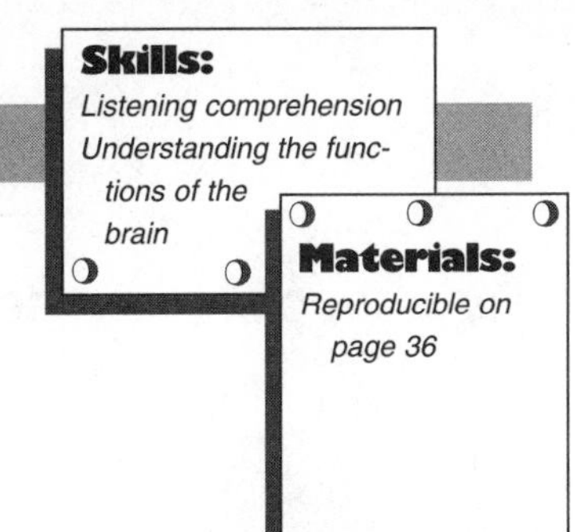


Optional Follow-Up Activity:

Under the picture of the brain write the numbers from 1 to 10. In each question, I will ask you to find the part of the brain that is responsible for a certain job in your body. You will need to write the number 1, 2 or 3 for your answer. Use your memory and the letters you have written in the drawing to help you figure out the answers.

1. Which part of the brain–number 1, 2 or 3–helps you write a letter?
2. Which part of the brain helps you keep your coordination and balance when you're riding a bicycle?
3. Which part of the brain helps you think of the answer to a math problem?
4. Which part of the brain makes you breathe?
5. Which part of the brain lets you smell pizza?
6. Which part of the brain controls your heartbeat?
7. Which part of the brain helps you coordinate your arms and legs during a game of tennis?
8. Which part of the brain allows you to read a book?
9. Which part helps you digest your food?
10. Which part of the brain helps you feel a sharp needle?

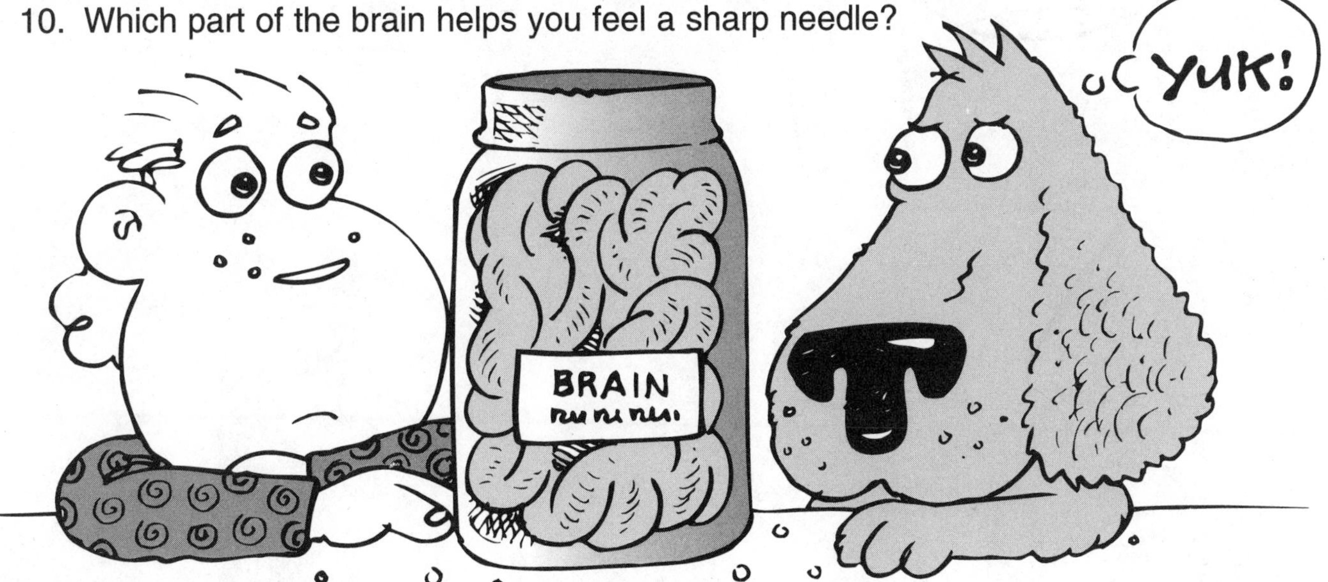

# Brain Bender

Reproducible for use with pages 34-35.

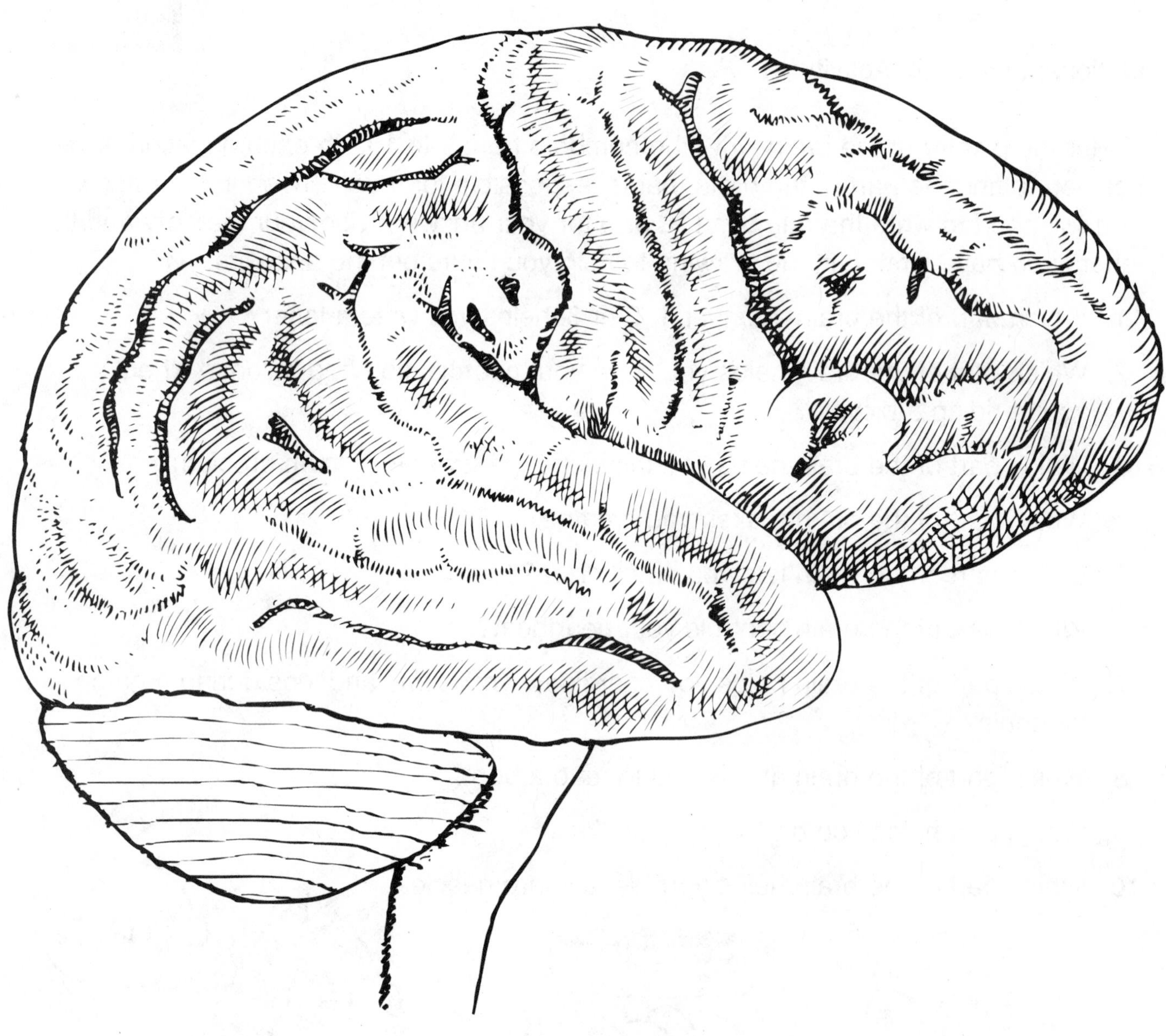

**Materials:**
*Lined paper*
*Pencil*

# Nutrition, Health and Safety

Write your name in the top right corner of your paper. Number your paper from 1 to 9.

For 1 and 2 I will name activities. If the activity that I read is good for your health and safety, write *yes* on your paper. If it is not good for your health and safety, write *no*.

1. Go swimming by yourself.
2. Eat a good breakfast.

For 3 and 4 I will read two food choices. Write the letter *A* or *B* for the food that is healthier for your body.

3. A. pop B. orange juice
4. A. hot dog B. chicken

For 5 and 6 I will read something that can be done for your teeth. If it is a good thing for your teeth, draw a smile face. If it is bad for your teeth, draw a frown.

5. Brush your teeth as quickly as you can.
6. Eat crunchy foods like apples and raw carrots.

For 7 I will read five actions. Write the number that tells how many of them are unsafe or unhealthy.

7. Crossing the street without checking for traffic.
   Taking candy from a stranger.
   Wearing a seat belt in the car.
   Eating a lunch of potato chips and cookies.
   Crossing the street only at the corner.

For 8 I will describe a job that someone has who helps keep people healthy. Write the name of this job on your paper by number 8.

8. This person takes care of your teeth. He checks to make sure your teeth are healthy, clean and growing properly. If this person finds a cavity, he will put a filling in it so it won't decay anymore.

For 9 unscramble these words to spell a safety rule:

9. PLAY MATCHES DON'T WITH

Finally, turn your paper over and follow these directions: Draw a large triangle. Draw lines across the triangle so that it is divided into four layers. This is a food pyramid that shows which foods you need in what amounts. You should have the smallest amounts of fats and sugar, so in the top layer of your triangle, write *F* for fat and *S* for sugar. In the bottom of the triangle draw some bread and macaroni. You should have the most foods from this bread and cereal group.

# Thumbs Up, Thumbs Down

Use as a Warm-Up for Part 4.

In this activity I am going to read you a list of several activities. If the activity that I list is good for your health and safety, give me a "thumbs up" sign. If it is bad for your health and safety, give me a "thumbs down" sign. If you're not sure, shrug your shoulders.

1. Look both ways before you cross the street.
2. Play with matches.
3. Eat a lot of junk food.
4. Learn your address and phone number.
5. Take candy from a stranger.
6. Wash your hands before eating.
7. Use another person's comb.
8. Eat fruits and vegetables.
9. Cough on someone's food.
10. Eat a good breakfast.
11. Get several hours of sleep each night.
12. Go swimming by yourself.

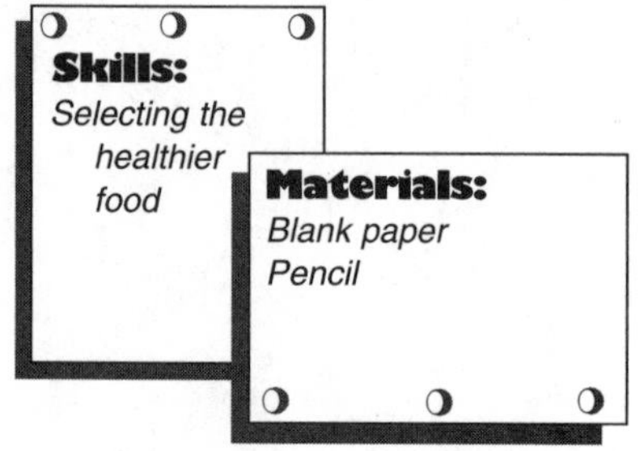


# Right Choices

Number your paper from 1 to 10. For each number, I will read two foods. Pick the one that's healthier and write its letter, *A* or *B*. Remember to choose the food that's low in fat and sugar and that's fresh. Write your name in the top left corner of your page.

1. A. pop B. orange juice
2. A. baked potato B. potato chips
3. A. cornflakes B. doughnut
4. A. cake B. pretzels
5. A. milk B. soft drink
6. A. broiled fish B. fish sticks
7. A. cookie B. apple
8. A. canned peas B. fresh broccoli
9. A. hot dog B. chicken
10. A. French fries B. carrot sticks

**Skills:**
*Recognizing good oral hygiene habits*

**Materials:**
*Blank paper*
*Pencil*

# Smile!

Do you know the right way to take care of your teeth so that you will have a bright, healthy smile? Let's find out! Number your paper from 1 to 14. For each number I will read something that can be done for your mouth. If this action is good for your teeth, draw a smile face by the number. If the action is bad for your teeth, draw a frown face by the number.

1. Visit the dentist every six months.
2. Eat a lot of candy, cake and other sugary foods.
3. Use a worn-out old toothbrush.
4. Floss your teeth.
5. Eat crunchy foods like apples and raw carrots.
6. Brush your teeth as quickly as you can.
7. Use a fluoride mouthwash.
8. Chew a lot of gum that contains sugar.
9. Visit the dentist only when your mouth hurts.
10. Clean your teeth properly, especially before going to bed.
11. Try to open cans and bottle tops with your teeth.
12. Bite down on unpopped kernels of popcorn.
13. Cooperate with the dentist during your exam.
14. Grind your back teeth together.

Now write the number 15 and write your name next to it.

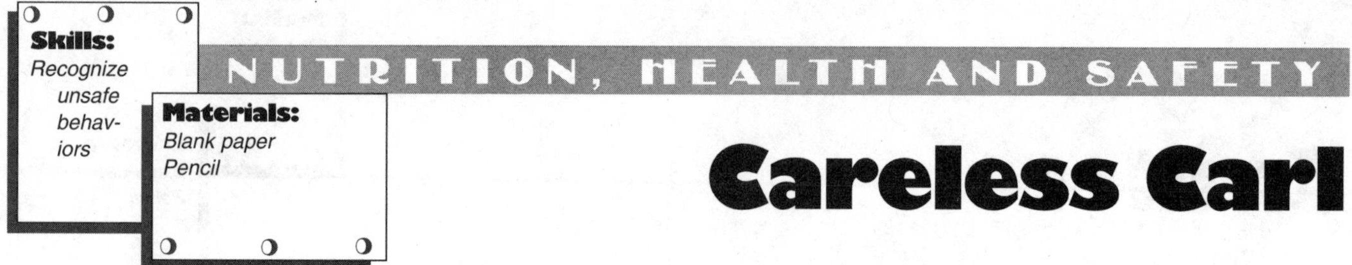




# Careless Carl

Fold your paper in half. Flatten it back out so you have a rectangle on the left and one on the right. Write your name at the top of the left half of your paper. Make a small box at the top of the right side of your paper.

Now I am going to read you a story about Careless Carl, a little squirrel who gets into mischief by doing things that are not safe. Make a tally mark in the box on your paper every time your hear that Carl is doing something unsafe or unhealthy. (Show students how to make tally marks if necessary.) When I'm done with the story, I will ask you to count the total number of unsafe or unhealthy things that Carl did in the story. I will also ask you to draw some pictures on your paper.

**Story:**

It was a beautiful fall day–just the kind of day when squirrels love to run around gathering acorns for winter. Careless Carl was excited as he woke up in his home in the hollowed out oak tree. He was so anxious to get to work that he decided to skip breakfast. He ran down the trunk of the tree and bounded across the street, without checking for traffic. He headed straight for his best buddy's tree house.

When he found his friend, Freddy, he invited him to go acorn gathering with him. Freddy agreed and they spent the morning working at Freddy's place. After a lunch of French fries and cupcakes, the squirrels decided to go over to Carl's tree to work. They darted between parked cars, out into the street and just escaped colliding with a delivery truck! Before the two reached Carl's oak tree, they stopped to talk to a stranger. The stranger's name was Boris, and he offered Carl and Freddy some delicious looking candy. Carl ate some, but Freddy didn't. Then Boris offered to take them in his car to a park loaded with lots of great playground equipment. Carl talked Freddy into going along. They got into the stranger's car. The squirrels were quickly on their way, before they could fasten their seat belts. On the way to the park, Carl and Freddy started thinking maybe they had made some mistakes.

Just then, while the car was stopped at a traffic light, Carl noticed flames coming from his favorite store, Nathan's Nut House. Fortunately, Boris let the squirrels out of the car, and Carl ran into the Nut House. He wanted to see if his good friend Nathan was still inside. Fortunately, a fire fighter saw Carl just inside the door and carried him back outside. Freddy and Carl walked slowly back toward home, glad to be safe but thinking of all the bad things that could have happened.

# Careless Carl

About two blocks from home, the squirrels saw a workman on a ladder outside Greta's Grocery. Carl noticed that the worker had dropped something on the ground. It was a pocketknife. So, trying to be helpful, Carl dashed under the ladder, picked up the knife by the handle and handed it back with the blade pointed at the worker.

Just then Freddy noticed some cups sitting on the sidewalk. Both squirrels darted closer to investigate the liquid inside the cups. They thought it looked and smelled like fruit juice. And since Carl was so thirsty, he drank a few swallows out of one of the cups. The squirrels continued the walk home. Just as they reached Carl's tree house, Freddy thought Carl didn't look too well. He helped Carl up the trunk of the tree into his safe, cozy house where the two squirrels told Carl's mother all about their dangerous day.

(Repeat story if necessary.)

Now, how many unsafe things did you count Carl doing? Write that number next to your box with tally marks.

Think back to one mistake that Carl made. What did he do wrong? What should he have done? Draw a picture on the left-hand side of your paper of one unsafe or unhealthy thing that Careless Carl did in the story. Then on the right side of your paper, draw a picture of what Carl should have done.

# Healthy Work

I have written the names of eight different kinds of workers on the board. Let's read these words together. I am going to tell you a little about each type of worker, and when I'm done I am going to ask you to draw a picture showing one of them at work.

1. A **doctor** examines patients who are sick and decides how to treat them so they will get better. How many of you have been to a doctor? Doctors also check healthy patients and make sure they are taking care of themselves properly. There are many kinds of doctors. Some treat just one part of the body such as the heart or the foot. Others work mainly on one disease such as cancer. Doctors spend a lot of time with patients; they also spend time researching information on diseases and treatments.
2. A **nurse** often helps a doctor. When you have a doctor's appointment, you may first see a nurse who checks your temperature, blood pressure, height and weight. Nurses can give shots. In hospitals they spend a lot of time taking care of patients and writing down information about the patients for the doctors.
3. A **dentist** takes care of your teeth. How many of you have been to a dentist? You probably already know that a dentist makes sure your teeth are growing properly and that you are taking good care of them. The dentist makes sure there are no cavities in your teeth. If there is, the dentist will have to put in a filling to keep your tooth from decaying more.
4. A **dental hygienist** usually works in a dentist's office. Often this is the person you see first. They hygienist cleans, scrapes and flosses your teeth. Sometimes this person takes X rays of your teeth.
5. A **pharmacist** follows doctors' instructions to make sure you get the right medicine in the right amount. The pharmacist can give you extra information about your medicine and answer your questions. Pharmacists will tell you the best time and the best way to take your medicine. They check to make sure you are not taking two medicines at the same time that don't work well together. Pharmacists often work in drugstores.

# Healthy Work

6. A **lab worker** studies blood and tissue from patients to try and learn what is making them ill. Lab workers study samples under microscopes. They perform tests and take notes on what they observe. The lab workers may never see the patient, but they provide important information to the doctor who is caring for the patient.

7. A physical **therapist** shows a patient what exercises can help them to recover. Sometimes after an injury or a stroke, a patient has to learn to do simple things all over again. A therapist can help someone learn to use a cane, a walker or a wheelchair. Or they can help a person learn to walk again. Therapists can help other patients avoid surgery by showing them ways to take care of their backs or necks. A therapist can work in a hospital, in an office, in a nursing home or in a patient's home.

6. An **X-ray technician** takes special pictures of parts of a patient's body. These pictures are called X rays. The pictures show doctors the inside of your body. X rays can show a doctor a broken bone or a problem in your lung. Technicians take the pictures, develop the pictures, study the pictures and then sometimes write a report about them for the doctor.

There are many more health care jobs, but for now we will stop with these eight. Both men and women can have any of these jobs. Which of the eight jobs that I read sound the most interesting to you? On your paper, draw a picture of you doing that job. Try to show the equipment you would use, the room where you'd be working and the other people with whom you would be working. Color your picture with your crayons. Write your name on the back of your picture.

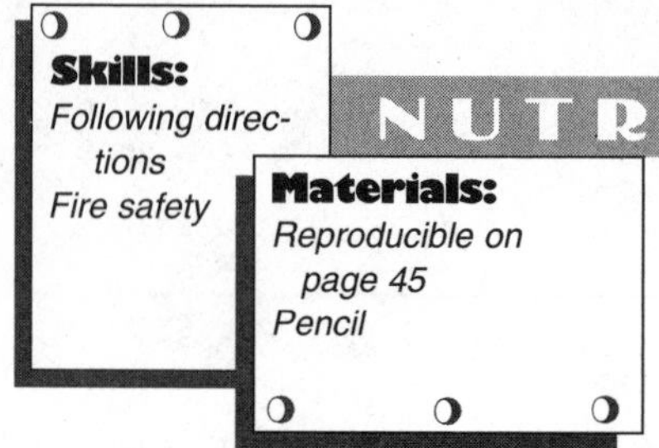




# Safety Sort-Out

In this activity I will give you a number of instructions about the list of words on your page. If you listen carefully and follow all the directions correctly, when we are done you will have an important rule about fire safety.

1. Draw a line through all the words that rhyme with *sun.*
2. Put an *X* on all the words that begin with the *th* sound.
3. In the first column, underline all the words that start with *G.*
4. Draw a line above the words that are names of animals.
5. Put an *X* on all the words that begin with the *B* sound.
6. Draw a line through any words that have a *W* in them.
7. Draw a wiggly line under the two words that rhyme with *past.*
8. Now look over all the words on your list. Circle the ones that have no marks by them.
9. Put a 1 above the word that is circled in the first row.
10. Put a 3 above the word that is circled in the second row.
11. Put a 4 above the word that is circled in the third row.
12. Put a 2 above the word that is left in the fourth row.
13. Now copy the numbered words into the matching numbered blanks. You should have a safety rule that tells you what to do if your clothes ever catch on fire.
14. Write your name under blank 4.

# Saftey Sort-Out

Reproducible for use with page 44.

| GO | STOP | RUN | BALL | THE |
|---|---|---|---|---|
| GIRL | BUN | AND | FAST | CAT |
| ROLL | WAS | THIS | DOG | LAST |
| FUN | BIG | THEY | DROP | WHEN |

______________ ______________ ______________ ______________

1 2 3 4

# Pyramid Pointers

During this activity we are going to complete a food pyramid. This pyramid was recommended by the federal government in 1992 as a guideline to a healthy diet. When yours is complete, you will have a picture to help you make good choices in the foods you eat.

1. Let's begin at the top of the pyramid. Notice this is the smallest portion of the pyramid; that means the types of food in this part, which are fats and sugars, should be the smallest part of our diet. The symbol for fats is a small circle, and the symbol of sugars is a small triangle. Draw several small circles and triangles in this part. In the box on the side that says *Key*, make a small circle by the word *fats*. Make a small triangle by the word *sugars*. This key will help you remember what the circles and triangles represent. We should eat only small amounts of fats and sugars each day.
2. Now let's move down to the second layer in the pyramid. Notice that there are two parts here–one on the left and one on the right. In the box on the left draw a glass of milk and a piece of cheese. In the blank next to this box write *2 dash 3*. This means you need to have 2 or 3 servings of these foods each day.
3. Next we'll complete the right-hand portion of the second layer. In this box draw an egg and a piece of meat. This will represent the foods that give us most of our protein, including meat, chicken, turkey, dry beans, eggs and nuts. In the blank next to this box write *2 dash 3*. This means you need to have 2 or 3 servings of these foods each day.
4. Now go to the third layer of the pyramid. Notice it is a little larger than the last layer, so that means you'll need a little more of these foods. In the box on the left side of the third layer, draw some peas and a carrot. This box will represent all vegetables, including potatoes, lettuce, beans, cabbage, beats, peas and carrots. In the blank next to this box write *3 dash 5*. This means you need to have 3 to 5 servings of vegetables each day.
5. In the box on the right side of the third layer, draw an apple and a pear. This box will represent all fruits, including oranges, peaches, bananas, grapes, pears and apples. In the blank next to this box, write *2 dash 4*. This means you need to eat 2 to 4 servings of fruit every day.
6. Finally, we move to the bottom layer in the food pyramid. It is the largest, so these are the foods that you need to eat the most. Draw some bread and a bowl of cereal in this box. This box represents all breads, cereals, rice, noodles, spaghetti, macaroni and other pastas. In the blank next to this box, write *6 dash 11*. This means you need to eat between 6 and 11 servings from this food group every day. Write your name under the last layer of the food pyramid.

# Pyramid Pointers

Reproducible for use with page 46.

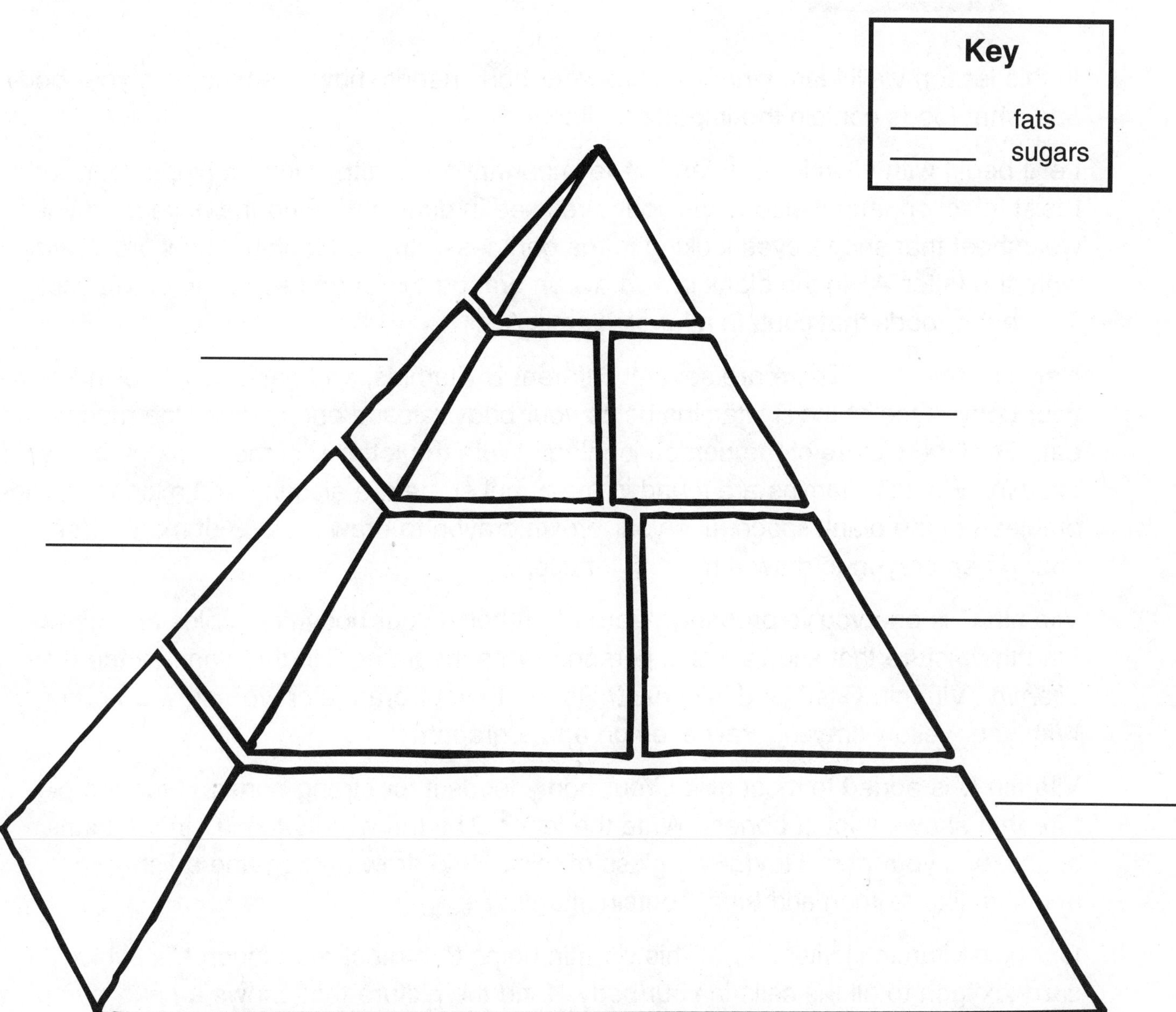

**Skills:**
*Sources and functions of vitamins*

**Materials:**
*Reproducible on page 49*
*Pencil*
*Crayons: orange, green, yellow, brown*

# Vitamins!

In this lesson we'll learn what vitamins your body needs, how vitamins help your body and what foods contain the important vitamins.

Let's begin with vitamin A. Vitamin A is important for healthy skin. It helps your body resist infection, and it also helps your eyes see in dim light. Find the picture on your worksheet that shows eyes looking in the darkness. In the blank by the word *vitamin*, write the letter *A*. In the blank box, draw an orange carrot and some green broccoli. These are foods that contain a lot of vitamin A.

Next is vitamin B. There are several different B vitamins, and each has its own job in your body. One of the B vitamins helps your body release energy from the food you eat. Find the picture of the person jogging. Write the letter *B* in the blank by the word *vitamin*. Most B vitamins are found in meat, but some are also in certain kinds of vegetables. In the blank space, use your brown crayon to draw a piece of meat. Use your green crayon to draw a head of lettuce.

Vitamin C is one you've probably heard of. It helps your body fight colds and germs. Find the picture that shows a sick person. Write the letter *C* in the blank by the word *vitamin*. Vitamin C is found in citrus fruits. With your orange crayon draw an orange. With your yellow crayon, draw a lemon and a grapefruit.

Vitamin D is added to most milk. Your body needs it for strong bones. Find the picture that shows a lot of bones. Write the letter *D* by the word *vitamin*. In the blank space, use your pencil to draw a glass of milk. Also draw an egg and a fish. Eggs and fish, like salmon and tuna, contain vitamin D.

Our next vitamin is vitamin E. This vitamin helps to protect red blood cells, which carry oxygen to all the cells in your body. Find the picture that shows a heart pumping blood. Write the letter *E* by the word *vitamin*. Vitamin E is found in vegetable oils, nuts and wheat germ. With your brown crayon, draw some nuts in the blank space.

Our last vitamin in this lesson is vitamin K which helps blood clot. This means when you are injured, you stop bleeding after a few minutes. Find the picture that shows an injury. Write the letter *K* in the blank. You don't need to draw the picture here because this is one vitamin that our body usually makes by itself.

Write your name at the top of your paper.

# Vitamins!

Reproducible for use with page 48.

| | | | |
|---|---|---|---|
| vitamin ____________ | | vitamin ____________ | |
| vitamin ____________ | | vitamin ____________ | |
| vitamin ____________ | | vitamin ____________ | |

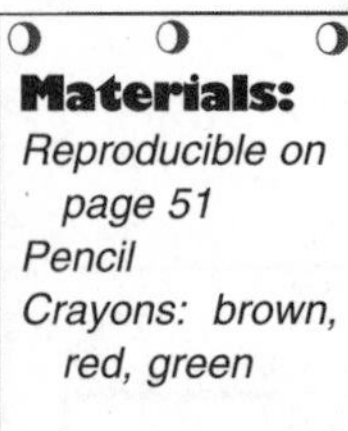

**Materials:**
*Reproducible on page 51*
*Pencil*
*Crayons: brown, red, green*



# Plants

For 1-3 I will read the name of a food. If the food comes from a plant, write *P*. If it comes from an animal, write *A*.

1. carrot sticks
2. orange juice
3. steak

It's pistil with an "i" not pistol with an "o."

Hey, I'm over here on this pistol.

4. In box 4 draw some soil or dirt. Draw two more things in nature that help a seed grow into a plant.

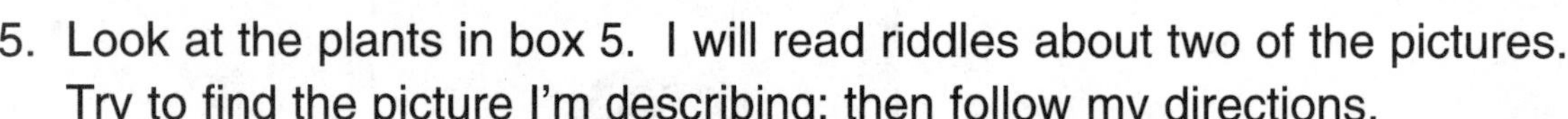

5. Look at the plants in box 5. I will read riddles about two of the pictures. Try to find the picture I'm describing; then follow my directions.
   Riddle 1: I'm an underground vegetable. I'm crunchy, red, round and a little bit "hot." If you've found me, use your red crayon to write your name in my box.
   Riddle 2: You eat lots of me every day in all kinds of foods. When I'm ripe I'm harvested by a large machine and ground up into flour. The flour is used in bread, crackers, cereal, cookies and noodles. If you've found me, circle me with your brown crayon.
6. In number 6 find the leaf that has lots of small leaves on one stem. It is a black locuts leaf. Underline it. Of the leaves that are left, find the two that match. They are elm leaves. Color them green.
7. In box 7 you'll see a tree. We get wood and paper from trees. Next to the tree draw three things made of wood or paper.
8. Look at the flower and words in box 8. Now find the thickest center part of the flower with the dots on top and the circles at the bottom. This center part of the flower is the pistil. Write the word *pistil* on the blank pointing to the pistil. At the top of the pistil is a sticky odd-shaped part called the stigma. Write the word *stigma* in the blank pointing to the stigma.

# Plants

Reproducible for use with page 50.

1. ______ 2. ______ 3. ______

4.

5.

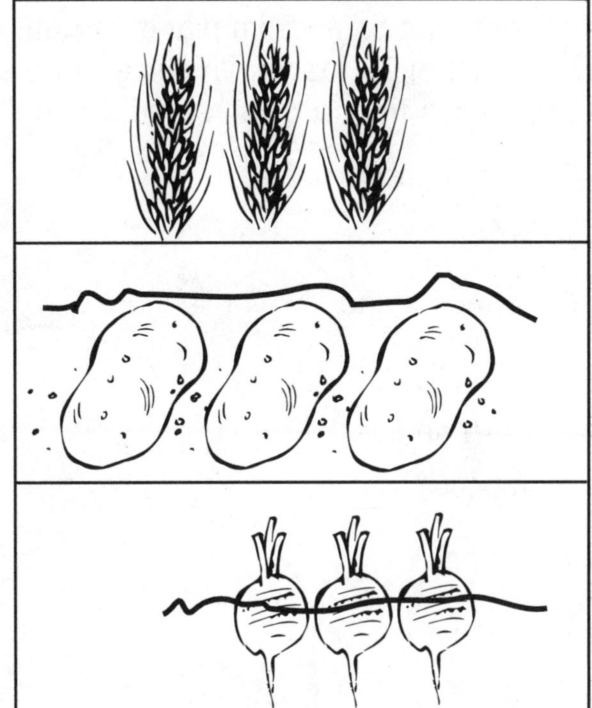

6.

7.

8.

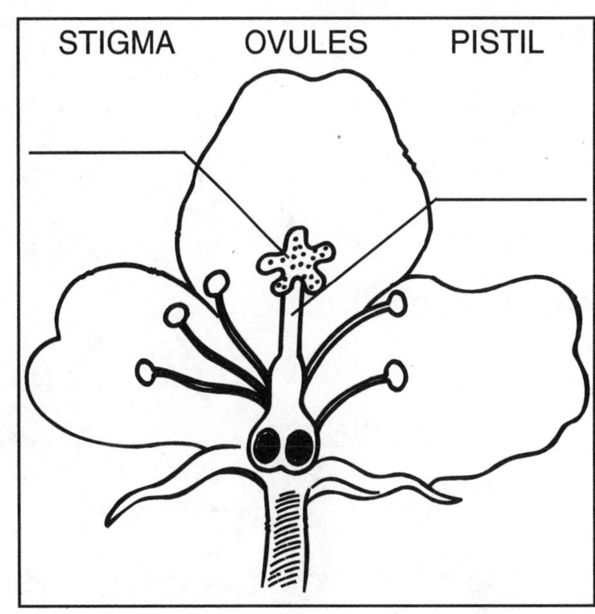

**Skills:**
*Recognizing source of common foods*

**Materials:**
*Students*

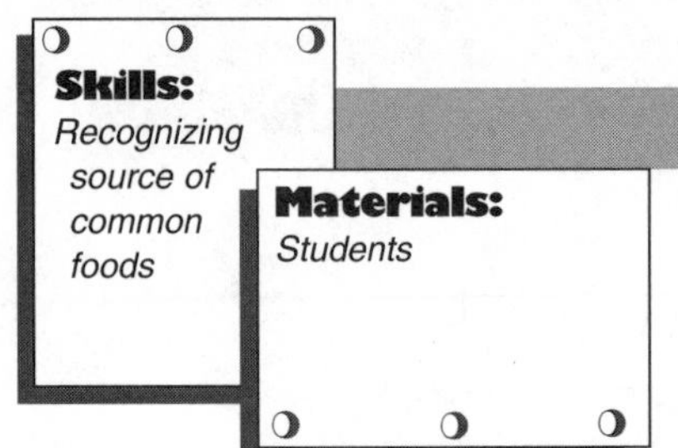

# Plant Food

Use as a Warm-Up for Part 5.

Lots of foods come from plants. Some of our food comes from animals. I am going to read a list of 20 foods. Think carefully about where we get each of these foods. If the food comes from a plant, stand up. If the food comes from an animal, sit down.

1. carrot sticks
2. milk
3. lettuce salad
4. apples
5. corn on the cob
6. bacon
7. grapes
8. bread
9. steak
10. cheese
11. broccoli
12. hamburger
13. tomato slices
14. lemon
15. eggs
16. French fries
17. orange juice
18. strawberry jam
19. ham
20. mashed potatoes

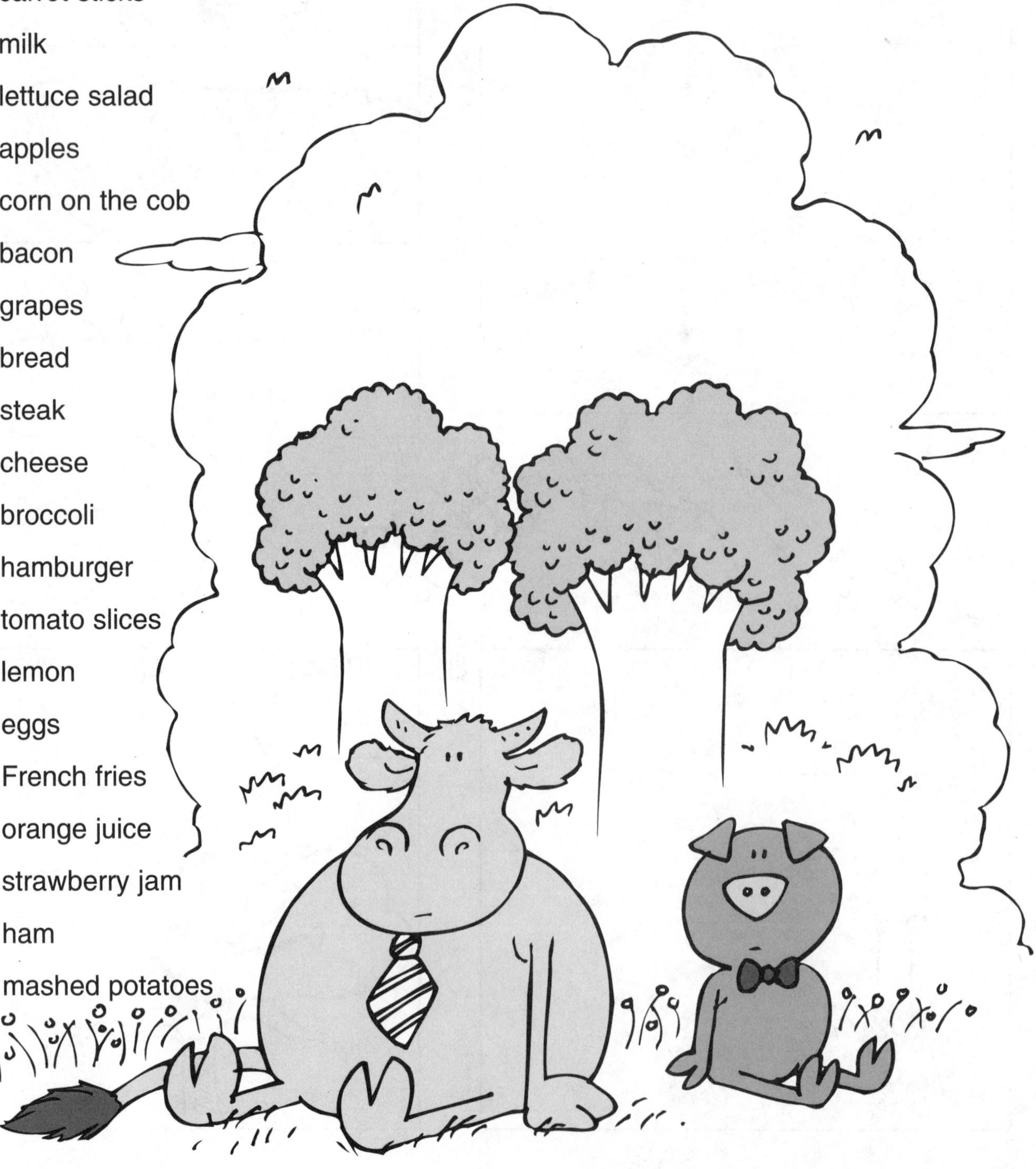

# Seed Draw

**Skills:**
*Drawing a cross-section of a seed and what the seed needs to grow*

**Materials:**
*Blank paper*
*Crayons: brown, green, yellow, blue*

Fold your paper in half lengthwise and in half again crosswise. Flatten your paper out so that you have four rectangles.

In the top left rectangle you will draw a picture that shows what a bean seed might look like on the inside. With your brown crayon, draw a large oval. Make your brown line thick and dark. This is called the seed coat. Near the top of the seed on the inside, draw two small green leaves. These leaves are the beginning of a new plant. Color the rest of the inside of the seed yellow. This shows the food that feeds the new plant as it starts to open.

In the other three boxes, you are going to draw things that this seed will need to grow into a healthy plant. Do you know what those things might be?

In the top right rectangle draw some brown soil. The roots of the new plant must grow down into the soil where they will take in water and minerals for food.

In the bottom left rectangle draw some blue clouds and rain. The rain will soak the seed and soften its seed coat.

In the bottom right rectangle draw the sun with your yellow crayon. The leaves of the new plant use the sun's energy for growth. Write your name in the box with the sun.

**Skills:**
*Identifying common food plants*

**Materials:**
*Reproducible on page 55*
*Crayons: red, brown, green, yellow, orange*

# Food Riddles

On your page are pictures of eight plants that we eat. I will read you riddles about seven of the pictures. When you've guessed which picture I'm talking about, you'll need to follow some directions.

Riddle 1: When I'm ripe I'm round, juicy and red. I'm used in juice, ketchup and spaghetti sauce. You can put a nice thick slice of me on your hamburger. If you've found me, color me red.

Riddle 2: You eat lots of me every day in all kinds of foods. When I'm ripe I'm harvested by a large machine and ground into flour. The flour is used in bread, crackers, cereal, cookies and noodles. If you've found me, circle me with your brown crayon.

Riddle 3: I grow underground. I'm very crunchy. You can eat me raw or cooked. Because I'm a dark yellow or orange color, I contain vitamins that are good for your eyesight. If you've found me, color my friends and me with an orange crayon.

Riddle 4: I'm a green crunchy, leafy vegetable. I'm eaten a lot in salads or on sandwiches. If you've found me, color me green.

Riddle 5: I'm an underground vegetable. I'm crunchy, red, round and a little bit "hot." If you've found me, use your red crayon to write your name in my box.

Riddle 6: I grow in tall green stalks above the ground, but I'm yellow. I'm a popular summertime treat. Some kinds of me are ground and used as feed for farm animals. If you've found me, color me yellow.

Riddle 7: I'm another underground food. You can eat me in lots of different ways–boiled, mashed, baked or fried. You can eat me with my skin on or off. If you've found my picture, underline it with your brown crayon.

You should have one food left. Do you know what it is called? With your green crayon, put the first letter of this food's name in its box.

# Food Riddles

Reproducible for use with page 54.

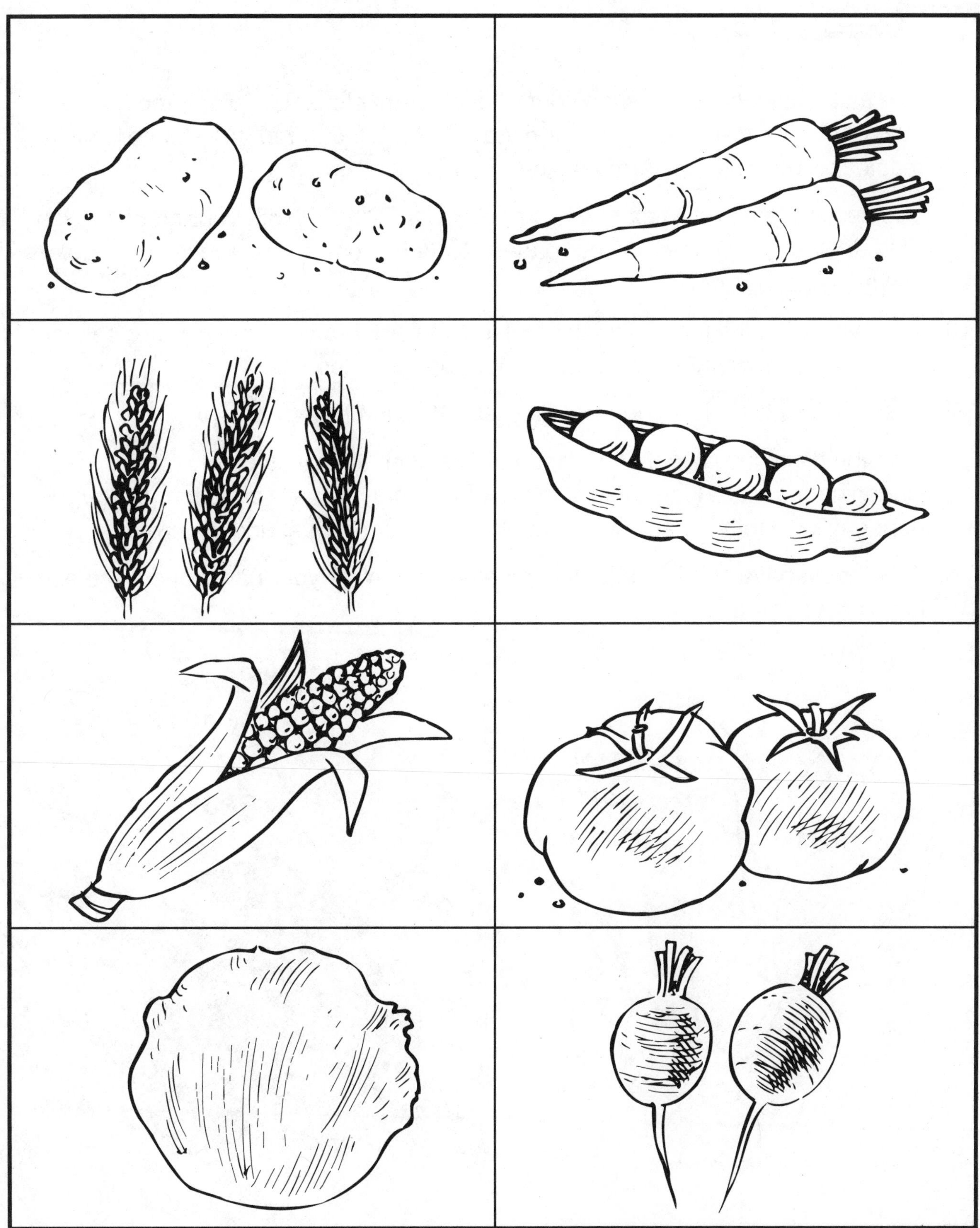

**Skills:**
*Recognizing different leaves*

**Materials:**
*Reproducible on page 57*
*Crayons: red, brown, green, black*

# Leaf Relief

1. The first leaf in the first row on your paper is a maple leaf. Color it red. Find one more maple leaf on your page. Color this one red, too. Under both maple leaves, write an *M* for maple.
2. The second leaf in the first row is a poplar leaf. Circle it with your green crayon. Find another poplar leaf on your page. Circle this one also. Above both poplar leaves, write a *P* for poplar.
3. The last leaf in the top row is an oak leaf. Color it brown. Find another oak leaf and color it brown, too. Write an *O* under both oak leaves.
4. Find a willow leaf. It is a long, skinny leaf. Color it green.
5. Find the black locust leaf. It is made of lots of small leaves on one stem. Underline the black locust leaf with your black crayon. At the bottom of your paper, draw another black locust leaf like the one you just underlined.
6. You should have one leaf left. It is an elm leaf. Write your name under the elm leaf with your red crayon.

# Leaf Relief

Reproducible for use with page 56.

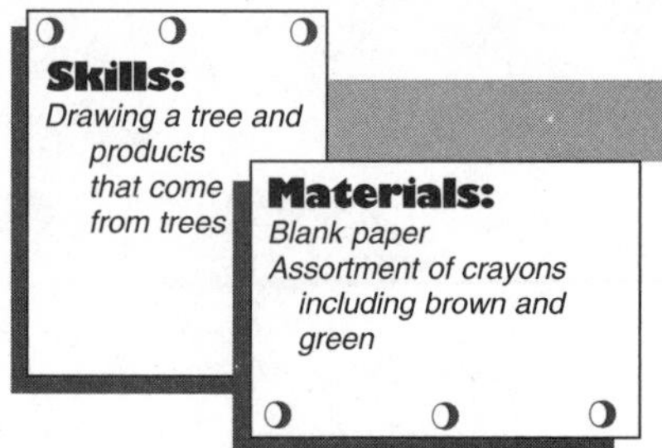




# Tree Time

Turn your paper so it is wide and short. On the left side of your paper, draw a tree following these directions:

Leave an inch or two of space at the bottom of your paper blank for now. Use your brown crayon to draw a nice thick tree trunk. Add some branches to the top of the trunk. Below the trunk where you left the space, draw some roots on the tree growing beneath the ground. Color in the trunk, branches and roots.

With your green crayon, add lines to show grass growing around the trunk of the tree. Also add a lot of green leaves to the tree. Write your name above the tree.

Do you know which fruits grow on trees? A few are apples, cherries, peaches, pears, plums, oranges, lemons, bananas and apricots. Draw three of these fruits in the middle of your paper.

Do you know what we make from trees? The wood is used to build our homes, desks, tables, chairs. Other furniture comes from trees. Paper is made from trees. On the right side of your paper, draw three things made of wood or paper.

**Skills:**
*Learning how seeds are spread*

**Materials:**
*Blank paper*
*Pencil*

# Scattered Seeds

Fold your paper in half and then flatten it out so you have a top half and bottom half. After you listen to this lesson, I will ask you to draw three parts of it, using the front and back of your paper.

New seeds grow inside of almost all plants. As the seeds become larger, a fruit or pod grows around them to protect them. When the fruit or pod ripens, it breaks open. Then the seeds are ready to grow into new plants.

But how do these seeds get planted? I will tell you six of the ways this happens. Listen closely, because you will be drawing pictures about some of these ways in a minute.

1. Some seeds just fall to the ground right at the base of the plant they grew on.
2. Some seeds fall into streams, rivers, lakes or the ocean. They travel with the water until they stick to dirt somewhere along the shore.
3. Some seeds are spread by birds. As birds eat berries from plants, they sometimes drop the seeds from the berries on the ground.
4. Animals also help spread seeds. They hide nuts and acorns in the ground which later grow into plants and trees.
5. The wind scatters some seeds, especially ones that have “fluff” on them and ones that have “wings” that spin as they fall.
6. Finally, people plant seeds in their yards and gardens. People plant seeds that someone else has grown or gathered and then sold in stores.

Let’s review these six ways in which seeds can be spread. (Briefly summarize.)

Now let’s go back to your paper. In each half of the front of your paper, draw one of the ways I mentioned that seeds are spread. On the back of your paper, draw a third way in the top box. In the bottom box on the back, draw a picture of your favorite plant. Write your name in this box.

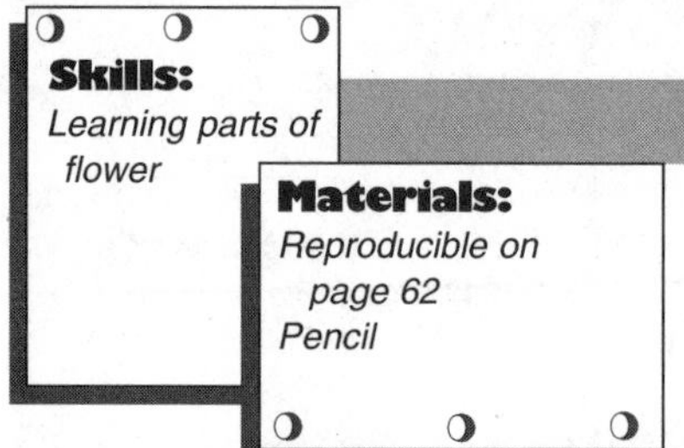




# Flower Parts

Many plants grow flowers, and flowers are where most seeds begin. Your worksheet shows different parts of a flower. As you listen to this lesson, you'll learn how a seed begins to grow. You'll also be given instructions to follow. The words you'll need are listed at the top of your page in the word bank. Let's read them together now. (Read word bank aloud with class.)

First let's label one of the flower petals. Your flower has three large petals. The petals are the colored parts that make up the blossom. Write the word *petal* above the petal on the left.

Next we will label the stem. The stem is the long thin tube that connects the flower to the leaves and roots. Write the word *stem* to the right of the stem near the bottom of your page.

Now find the thickest center part of the flower with the dots on top and the circles at the bottom. This center part of the flower is the pistil. Write the word *pistil* on the blank pointing to the pistil.

At the top of the pistil is a sticky odd-shaped part called the stigma. Write the word *stigma* in the blank pointing to the stigma.

At the bottom of the pistil are small circles that represent tiny egg cells. These are called ovules. Write the word *ovules* in the blank pointing to the round parts at the bottom of the pistil.

# Flower Parts

The thinner parts of the flower around the pistil are the stamens. Your picture shows five stamens. Write the word *stamen* in the blank pointing to the stamen on the right.

On the top of the stamen is yellow powder called pollen. This pollen has to get from the stamen to the stigma before a seed can begin to grow. Find these parts on your picture.

When the pollen is moved, this is called pollination. Do you know how flowers are pollinated? Sometimes the wind blows pollen from flower to flower. Sometimes bees and hummingbirds help pollinate. As they visit flowers gathering nectar, the pollen sticks to their body. Then they carry that pollen to the next flower where it comes off the animal and goes onto the pistil of the second flower. Draw a bee around your flower to remind you of pollination.

When a pollen grain from a flower lands on the pistil of the same kind of flower, it grows a long tube through the pistil into an ovule. This is the start of a seed. Draw a line to represent this tube. It starts at the top of the pistil and goes to the bottom of the pistil into an ovule.

Write your name at the top of your paper.

# Flower Parts

Reproducible for use with pages 60-61.

**Word Bank**

petal stem pistil stigma ovules stamen

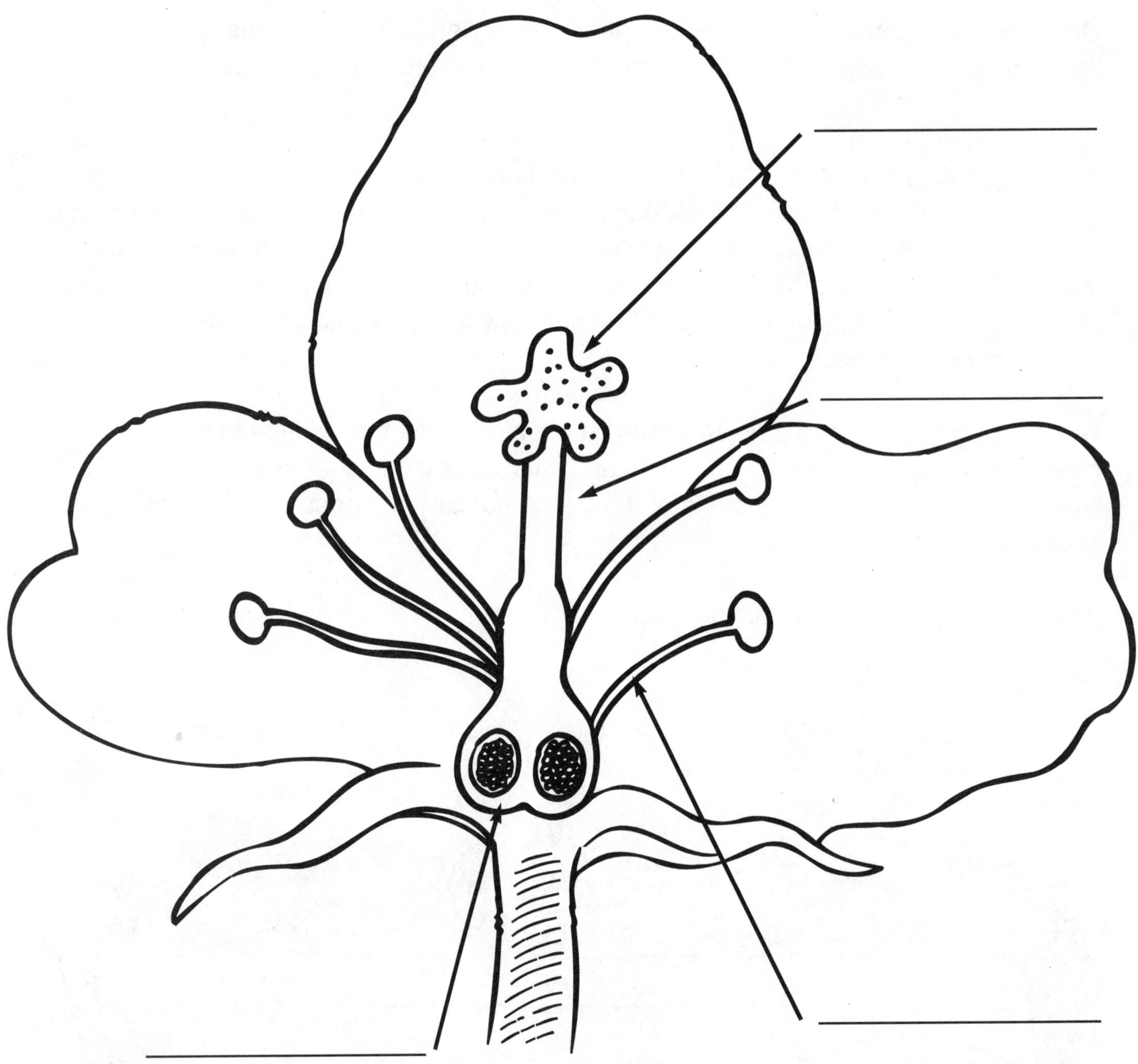

# Animals

**Materials:**
*Reproducible on page 64*
*Pencil*

Look at the animals on the first line on your paper. I will read a riddle about one of them. Circle the animal that it is talking about in this riddle: I have eight legs. I eat other bugs. I spin webs.

For numbers 2 and 3 on your paper, I will read three letters. In the first blank by each number, write the letters. In the second blank, write the name of an animal you can spell by rearranging the three letters.

2. w o c
3. a t b

For numbers 4, 5 and 6, I will read the name of an animal. If the animal lives mostly on land, write *L*. If it lives only in the water, write *W*. If the animal lives in both, write *B*.

4. monkey
5. penguin
6. octopus

For numbers 7 and 8, I will read you a few sentences about an animal called a dingo. Then I will ask you some questions.

Dingoes are wild dogs that live in the country of Australia. They live in forests, in mountains, along the coasts and on grassy, flat plains. The dingoes that live in the hottest, driest parts of Australia are mostly nocturnal. That means they are most active at night. During the day, they stay out of the hot sun.

7. Are dingoes wild or tame? Write *W* for wild or *T* for tame.
8. Some dingoes are nocturnal. What does this mean? Write *D* if it means they are active during the day. Write *N* if it means they are active during the night.

Look at the animals in line 9. Listen to these clues to discover which of these is the mystery animal. CLUES: I don't have tusks. I don't have wings. I don't have four legs. When you've found the mystery animal, circle it.

For 10 and 11, I will read you the name of an animal. If it is a mammal, write *M*. If it is reptile, write *R*.

10. turtle
11. ape

For 12 and 13, I will read three animals. Each will have a letter–*A*, *B* or *C*. Write the letter of the animal that is *not* a bird.

| | | |
|---|---|---|
| 12. A. cricket | B. crow | C. grosbeak |
| 13. B. gull | B. pheasant | C. moth |

Write your name at the top of the page.

# Animals

Reproducible for use with page 63.

1.   

2. ____________ ____________ 3. ____________ ____________

4. ____________ 5. ____________ 6. ____________

7. ____________ 8. ____________

9.

10. ____________________ 11. ____________________

12. ____________________ 13. ____________________

**Skills:**
*Naming insects from clues*

**Materials:**
*Students*

# Riddles That Will Bug You!

Use as a Warm-Up for Part 6.

I will read you some riddles. Your job is to figure out what kind of insect or creature is talking in the riddle. When you think you know the answer, stand up. Wait until I call on you before you answer.

1. I have spots. Even if I am a male, I am still a "lady."
2. I have stripes. I have wings. I have a stinger.
3. I am a bright light in the night. I fly.
4. I have eight legs. I eat other bugs. I spin webs.
5. I am very, very slow. My body is moist and sticky. The shell I carry on my back keeps me from drying out.
6. I have wings. I have big eyes. I buzz around your house.
7. I can have bright, pretty colors. I used to be a caterpillar.
8. I have strong back legs that help me hop, hop, hop in the grass. I am green like the grass.
9. I am not a butterfly, but I look like one. I am attracted to bright lights at night.
10. I have large eyes and very large wings. I am much bigger than a regular fly. I lay my eggs in the water.

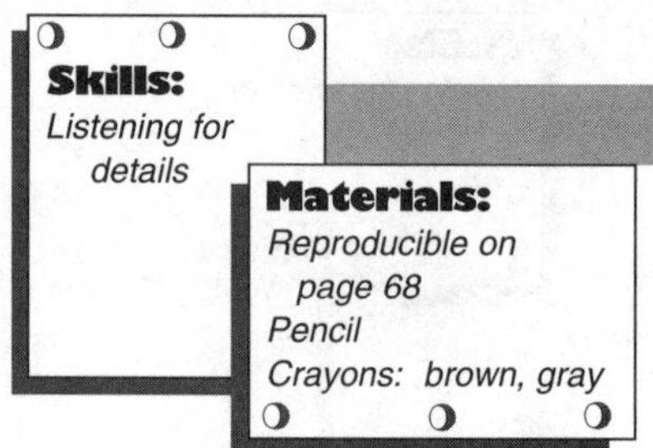




# Tundra Time

The tundra is a very cold area near the Arctic Ocean. In winter the temperature may drop as low as -60°F (-15°C), and the sun may not shine for several days at a time. Much of the ground is permanently frozen, and less rain falls in the tundra than in some deserts. But in spite of the very cold climate, many animals are able to live in the tundra. On your worksheet you will see pictures of six of these animals. As I tell you a few facts about each animal, find that animal on your worksheet and follow the directions I give you.

1. First find the musk-ox. It is a large beast with a thick, dark brown shaggy coat. Why do you think its coat is so thick? That's right–to protect it from the bitter cold. Find the picture of the musk-ox and color its coat brown while I tell you a little more about it. The musk-ox has short legs, but it can grow to be huge. Some weigh as much as 900 pounds (405 kg)! The musk-ox has broad horns that curve downward. Musk-oxen live in herds of 20 to 100 animals. When they are under attack, they form a circle with their horns outward and with their young inside the circle.
2. Now find the walrus. The walrus is closely related to the seal. Did you ever notice that walruses do not have ears? They do have long tusks, however. Notice on your picture the walrus is missing his tusks. Use your pencil to draw in two long tusks coming out of the walrus's mouth. Walruses sometimes use their tusks to climb up onto the ice, to fight their enemies and to stir up clams and other food off the bottom of the ocean. Walruses grow to be even more enormous than the musk-ox. The males can be as long as 12 feet (3.65 m) and can weigh up to 3,000 pounds (1.35 t)!
3. Now find the wolf. This wolf that lives in the tundra is called a gray wolf. Color the wolf on your paper with your gray crayon. The gray wolf is also called the timber wolf. It is the largest member of the dog family. The gray wolf hunts other mammals for food. Sometimes if follows polar bears to eat the "leftovers" of what a polar bear hunts and eats.

# Tundra Time

4. Can you find the Arctic fox? It is smaller than the wolf. The Arctic fox has a brownish coat in the summer, which turns white in winter to help it hide in the snow. Its coat is very thick and its ears are short and very furry. The Arctic fox loses very little body heat because of its thick coat. Write your name under the Arctic fox.

5. Now find the seal. Seals like to eat fish. With your pencil, draw a fish in the mouth of the seal. Seals swim very well underwater, but they have a harder time moving across land. The hind limbs (or legs) of most seals are permanently turned backward to help the seal get across land. The seal has to wriggle, roll or slide whenever possible. Seals are a favorite food of the polar bears.

6. Lastly, let's talk about the polar bear. It should be the only remaining picture on your page. Like the Arctic fox, the polar bear is white so it is not easily seen in the snow of the tundra. Polar bears like to hunt seals and walruses for food. With your pencil, draw a line from the polar bear to the walrus. Draw another line from the polar bear to the seal. Polar bears build up layers of fat that help them survive the long winter.

Now turn your paper over. Try to draw your own picture of one of the tundra animals we've just studied. Write your name under the picture.

# Tundra Time

Reproducible for use with pages 66-67.

**Skills:**
*Spelling 3-letter animal names*

**Materials:**
*Lined paper*
*Pencil*

# Animal Trios

Write your name at the top of your paper. Number your paper from 1 to 15. By each number, write the three letters I will read you. Then try to rearrange those letters to spell an animal name. Write the name of the animal on the same line next to the scrambled letters. (Teacher: You may want to do the first one together.)

1. w o c
2. i g p
3. d g o
4. e l e
5. y f l
6. a t b
7. p a e
8. e b e
9. t a c
10. t r a
11. l w o
12. x f o
13. n t a
14. k y a
15. b c u

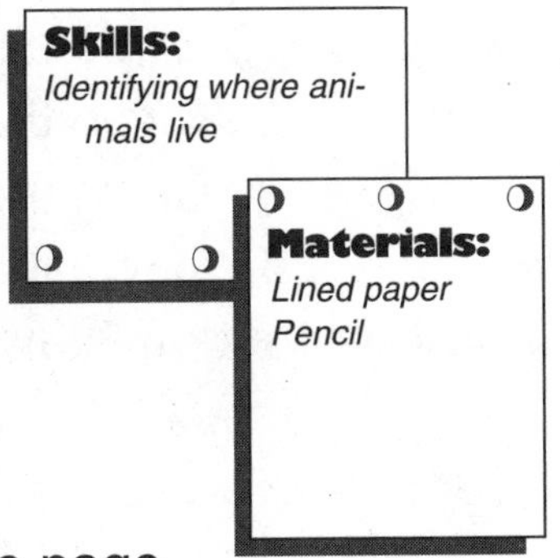


# Wetlands

Number your paper from 1 to 15. Write your name at the top of the page. In this lesson, I want you to think about what you already know about several animals. For each number on your paper, I will say the name of an animal. If the animal lives only on the land, write *L*. If the animal lives only in the water, write *W*. If the animal lives in both, write *B*. If you're not sure, put a question mark, and we'll talk about the correct answers at the end of the lesson.

1. horse
2. octopus
3. salamander
4. goldfish
5. zebra
6. crocodile
7. whale
8. monkey
9. frog
10. seal
11. cat
12. dolphin
13. penguin
14. pig
15. seahorse

**Skills:**
*Identifying various animal characteristics, Logic*

**Materials:**
*Reproducible on page 71*
*Crayons: blue, red, green*

# Mysterious Animals

Set 1: I am going to read you a set of clues to help you discover a "mystery" animal. With your blue crayon, underline animals following these directions:

1. Underline every animal with wings.
2. Underline every animal with one or more stripes.
3. Underline any animal with tusks.
4. Underline every animal with four legs.
5. Underline any animal with fins.

The mystery animal is the one left with no underlining. Put a number 1 above this animal with your blue crayon.

Set 2: Now we'll find another mystery animal on this same page. This time use your red crayon to follow the directions:

1. Circle all the insects.
2. Circle the animals that start with the letter *S*.
3. Circle the two animals that spend most or all of their time in the water.
4. Circle the four animals you might see in cages at the zoo.

The second mystery animal is the one without a red circle. Put a 2 above this animal.

Set 3: Now we'll find a third mystery animal. These clues are a little different. You will have to listen carefully to decide which animals to cross out. Put a green *X* on any animals that fit the clues.

1. I am an animal who does not have four legs.
2. I have a trunk.
3. I have one or more stripes.
4. I have a mane.

The remaining animal is the third mystery animal. Put a green 3 above this animal. Write your name under the tiger.

# Mysterious Animals

Reproducible for use with page 70.

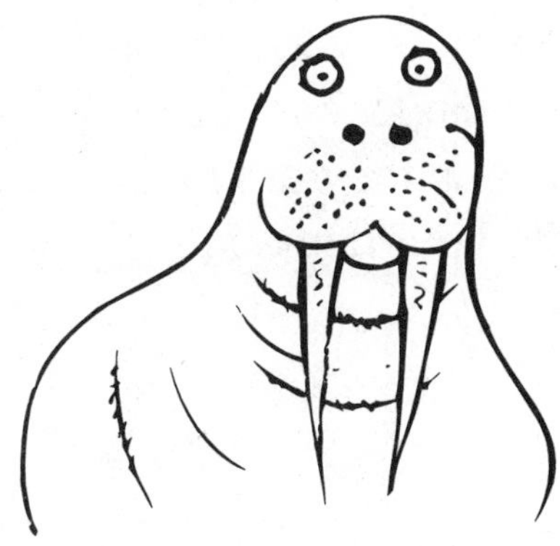

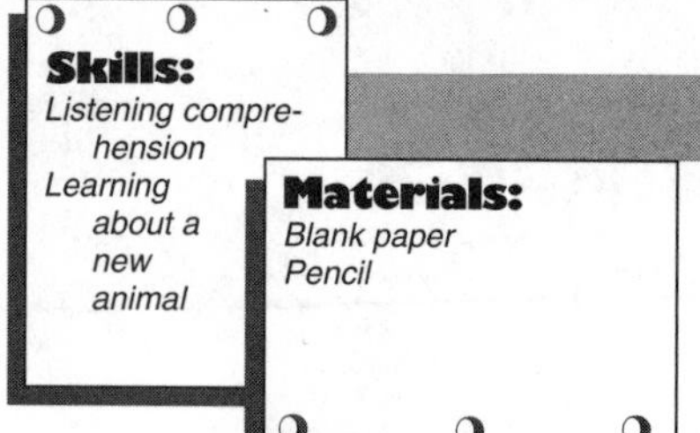


# Dingoes

Have you ever heard of an animal called the dingo? I am going to read some facts about dingoes. I want you to listen carefully so that you can draw a picture of a dingo. I will read the entire description before you draw; then I will read again while you draw.

Dingoes are wild dogs that live in Australia. They look much like our medium-sized pet dogs. Most dingoes are a yellowish color. A few are black or white. They usually have white feet and white hairs at the tip of their tail. They have pointed ears like a wolf, but their tail is not as fluffy as a wolf's tail. Dingoes have a larger head than our pet dogs with the same body size. They also have a longer nose and jaws and longer teeth.

Now, do you think you can draw a dingo? I'll read the description again slowly while you draw. Write your name in the top left-hand corner of your paper. (Repeat description, one sentence at a time, once or twice.)

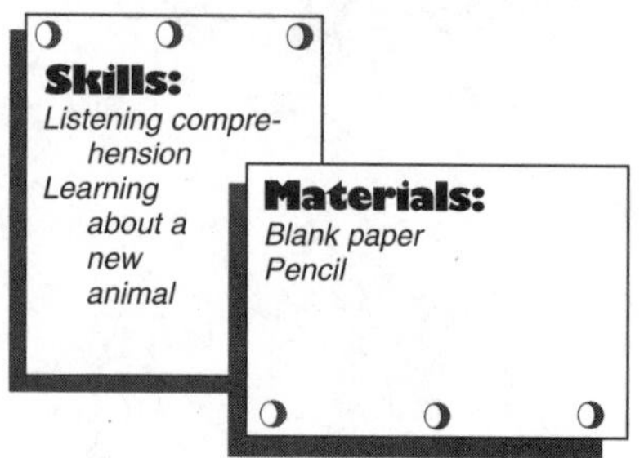


# More About Dingoes

Now that you know what a dingo looks like, let's learn more about how it lives. After I've read you these dingo facts, I will ask you to answer some questions, so please listen carefully.

Dingoes are wild dogs that live in the country of Australia. They are adaptable, which means they can adjust to living in many different places. In Australia, they live in forest, in mountains, along the coasts and on grassy, flat plains. The dingoes that live in the hottest, driest parts of Australia are mostly nocturnal. That means they are most active at night. During the day, they stay out of the hot sun. Write your name in the top right-hand corner of your paper.

# More About Dingoes

Dingoes may live alone or in groups with other dingoes. Female dingoes can have pups once a year. There are usually four or five pups in each litter. When the pups are three or four months old, they can live on their own. Dingoes in the wild may live to be eight or ten years old.

Like other dogs, the dingo is a hunter. It can run fast, and it has good eyesight and hearing. Some of the animals dingoes like to hunt are rabbits, lizards and small farm animals like calves and sheep.

Some dingoes are kept in Australia as pets. They are not truly tamed, however, and in some parts of Australia it is against the law to keep a dingo for a pet. Sheep ranchers in Australia do not like dingoes because they kill so many sheep. They even kill more than they can eat. In some places in Australia, however, dingoes are seen as helpers because they kill pests like rabbits and wild pigs.

1. In what country to dingoes live? Write *A* for Australia or *G* for Germany.
2. What kind of an animal is a dingo? Write *A* for ape or *D* for dog.
3. Are dingoes wild or tame? Write *W* for wild or *T* for tame.
4. Dingoes are adaptable. What does this mean? Write *L* if it means they can live in many different places or *E* if it means they eat a lot.
5. Some dingoes are nocturnal. What does this mean? Write *D* if it means they are active during the day. Write *N* if it means they are active during the night.
6. How old do wild dingoes get to be? Write *8* if it is eight to ten years. Write *20* if it is twenty to twenty-five years.
7. What do dingoes like to hunt? Write *M* for mice and monkeys or *R* for rabbits and sheep.
8. Are dingoes man's friend or enemy or both? Write *F* for friend, *E* for enemy or *B* if dingoes can be both friend and enemy to people.

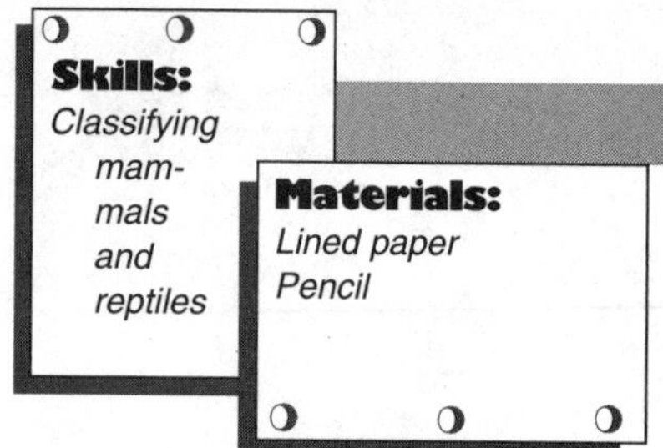




# Mammals and Reptiles

Do you know the differences between mammals and reptiles? In this lesson you will learn about some of them. I will also ask you to figure out in which of these two groups several animals belong.

First, let's talk about mammals. Mammals are animals with hair or fur on their bodies. Humans are mammals. So are monkeys and horses. Sometimes you can't see the hair on a mammal's body; for example, an elephant doesn't look furry, but it is a mammal. Mammals are also warm-blooded. That means they can keep their body temperature the same, even in different surroundings. Mammals also give birth to their babies, instead of hatching them from eggs like birds and snakes. Mother mammals feed their young special milk made inside their bodies.

Now we'll discuss reptiles. Most reptiles have scaly skin instead of the furry skin of mammals. Usually their young hatch from eggs instead of being born live from the mother's body. Reptiles are cold-blooded which means their bodies change temperature as their environment changes. Most reptiles crawl on the ground, like snakes or have very short legs, like crocodiles.

Next write your name at the top of your paper. Number the lines on your paper from 1 to 14. I will read you a list of fourteen animals. You need to decide if each one is a mammal or a reptile. If it is a mammal, write *M* on your paper by that number. If it is a reptile, write *R* on your paper. (Teacher: You may wish to do the first one or two together.)

1. ape
2. snake
3. rabbit
4. dog
5. lizard
6. sheep
7. deer
8. turtle
9. cat
10. alligator
11. bear
12. horse
13. chameleon
14. cow

# Bird Brains

**Skills:**
*Identifying different birds by name*

**Materials:**
*Lined paper*
*pencil*

How many different kinds of birds do you know? Number your paper from 1 to 12. For each number I will name three animals. Each will have a letter–*A*, *B* or *C*. Write the letter of the animal that is *not* a bird. If you're not sure of the right answer, make the best guess and we'll go over the right answers together at the end of the lesson.

| | | | |
|---|---|---|---|
| 1. | A. wren | B. hare | C. emu |
| 2. | A. sparrow | B. moray | C. eagle |
| 3. | A. boa | B. nuthatch | C. swallow |
| 4. | A. warbler | B. cardinal | C. mole |
| 5. | A. mink | B. falcon | C. dove |
| 6. | A. heron | B. robin | C. ermine |
| 7. | A. bat | B. duck | C. oriole |
| 8. | A. owl | B. skunk | D. woodpecker |
| 9. | A. turkey | B. eel | C. quail |
| 10. | A. gull | B. pheasant | C. moth |
| 11. | A. cricket | B. crow | C. grosbeak |
| 12. | A. swift | B. bison | C. pheasant |

Write your name under number 12.

(Teacher: This lesson can be adapted to other types of animals. Your students may want to learn about the "non-bird" animals named in this lesson.)

# Answer Key

## Pre/Posttest, Part 1, page 2

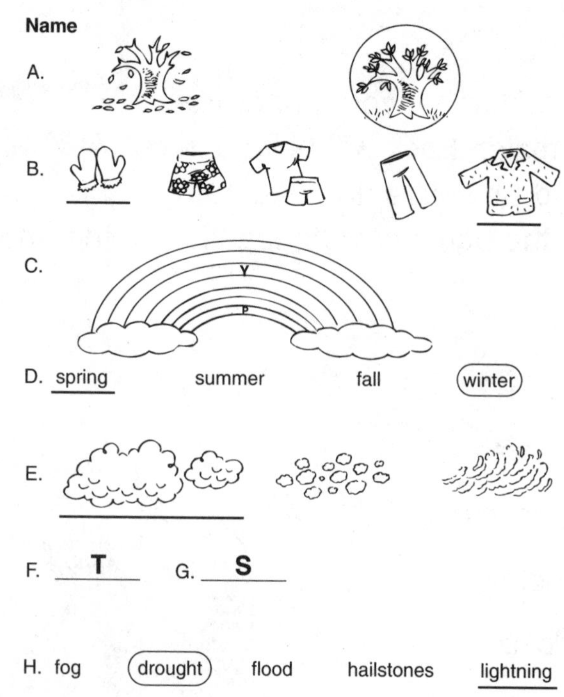


## Dressing for the Weather, page 5

G = green R = red
Y = yellow B = blue

## The Colors of the Rainbow, page 6

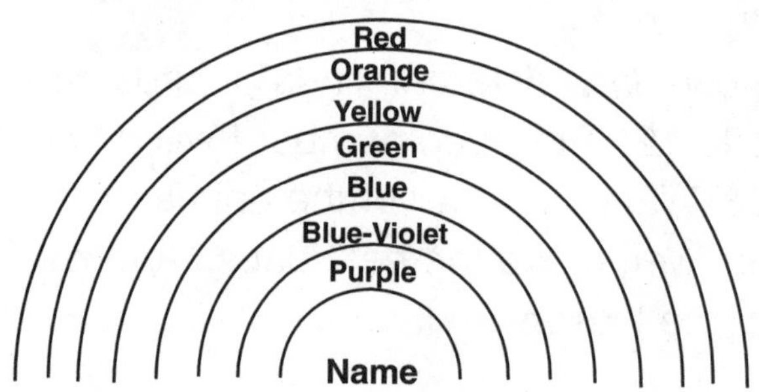


## Which Season? page 7

1. Name
2. winter
3. summer
4. spring
5. fall
6. winter
7. spring
8. fall
9. summer
10. fall
11. winter
12. spring
13. fall
14. fall
15. winter

## Cloud Cover, page 9

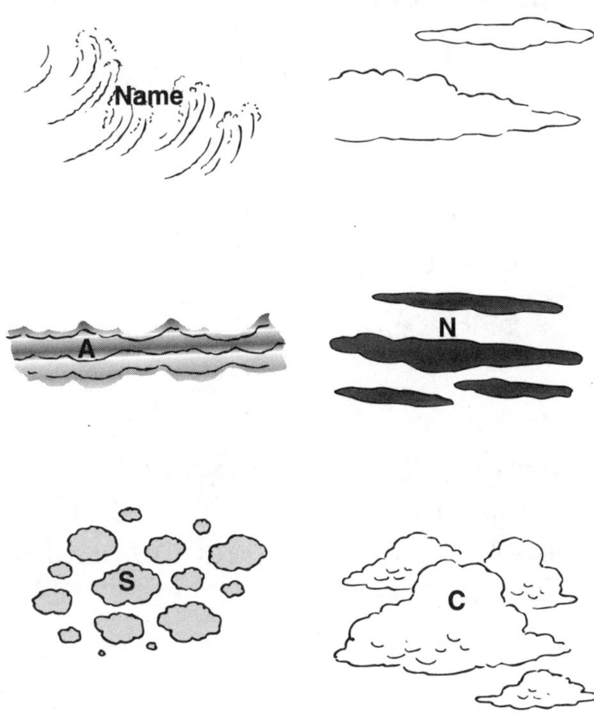


Back: Summer scene with cumulus clouds

## Higher or Lower? pages 10-11

Name in top left corner.

1. L
2. A
3. O
4. S
5. F
6. V
7. H
8. C
9. R
10. D
11. M
12. B
13. M
14. L
15. S

## Weather Words, page 12

Name in top right corner.

1. air
2. rainbow
3. dew
4. drought
5. tornado
6. hailstones
7. lightning
8. fog
9. smog
10. flood
11. snowflakes
12. frost

## Pre/Posttest, Part 2, page 14

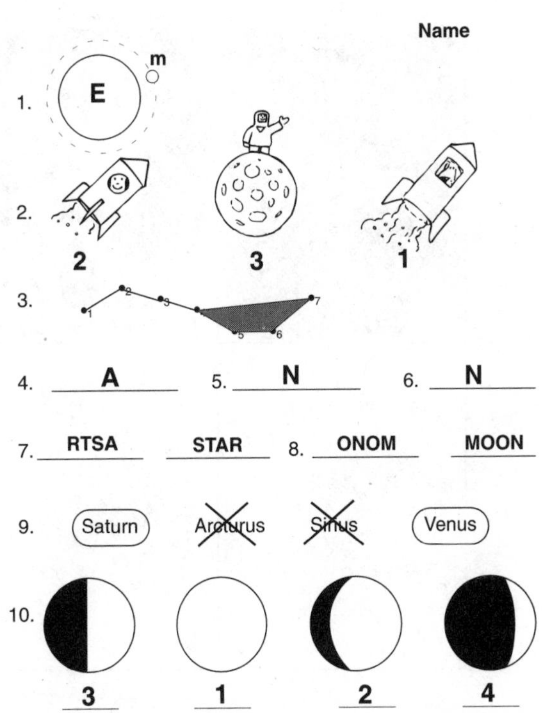

## Space Sketch, page 15

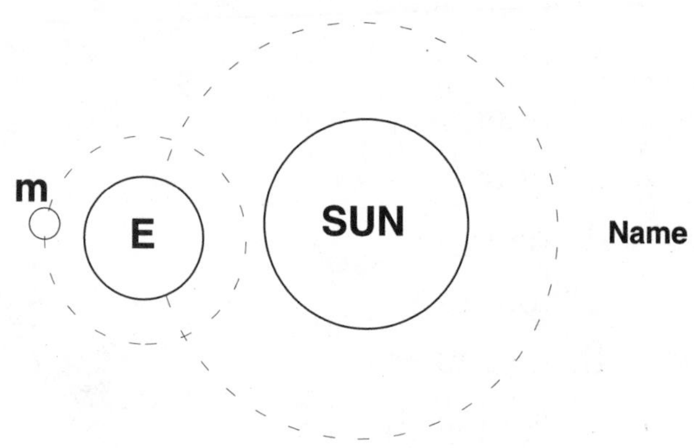


## Space Sequence, page 17

## The First Space Traveler, pages 18-19

1. D
2. L
3. O
4. S
5. S
6. P

Drawing of what the *Sputnik 1* satellite may have looked like. Name should be written under the picture. (Drawings will vary.)

## Star Dots, page 21

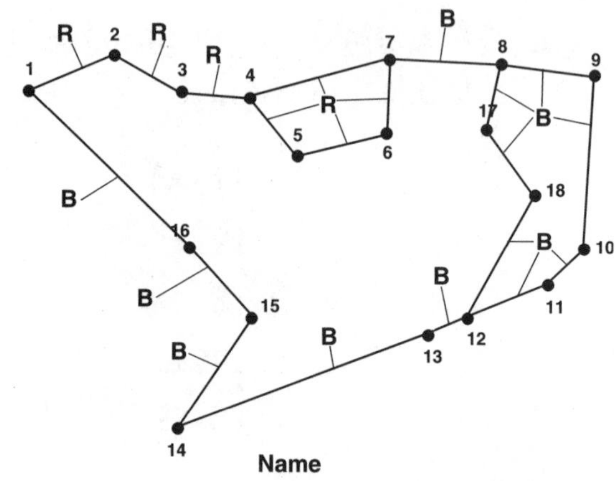

## Skyview, page 22

Name in top right corner.

1. N
2. A
3. N
4. N
5. A
6. A
7. N
8. N
9. N
10. A
11. N
12. A

## Planets and Stars, page 23

1. P
2. P
3. S
4. P
5. S
6. P
7. P
8. P
9. P
10. S
11. S
12. P
13. S
14. P
15. S

Name

## Space Scramble, page 22

Name in top left corner.

1. STAR
2. MOON
3. VENUS
4. SUN
5. MARS
6. PLUTO
7. EARTH
8. JUPITER
9. COMET
10. DIPPER

## Moon Mix-Up, page 25

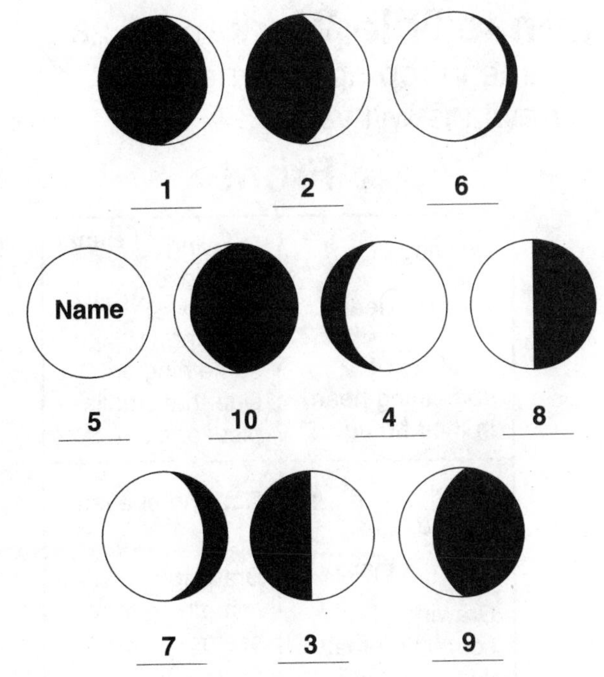

## Pre/Posttest, Part 3, page 26

1. Drawing of a nose and beside it a drawing of something they smell outside.

   (Drawings will vary.)
2. A.
3. C.
4. Drawing of an arm from the shoulder to the fingers with an *E* labeling the elbow and a *W* labeling the wrist.
5. Drawing of a head with a line showing the location of the mandible.
6. L
7. C
8. yes
9. no

Name

## "Sense"ible Work, page 28

Name in top right corner.
Drawings will vary.

### Front

| | |
|---|---|
| Drawing of an ear. **hear** Drawing of something heard in their home. | Drawing of a nose. **Name** **smell** Drawing of something outside that smells pleasant. |
| Drawing of a tongue. **taste** Drawing of something that tastes sweet. | Drawing of eyes. **see** Drawing of something they see from their seat. |

### Back

**touch**

Drawing of something that would feel sharp and someone touching it. (Drawings will vary.)

## What's Not Right? page 29

Name in top left corner.

1. C.
2. B.
3. A.
4. C.
5. B.
6. C.
7. A.
8. B.
9. A.
10. C.

## Body Parts, page 30

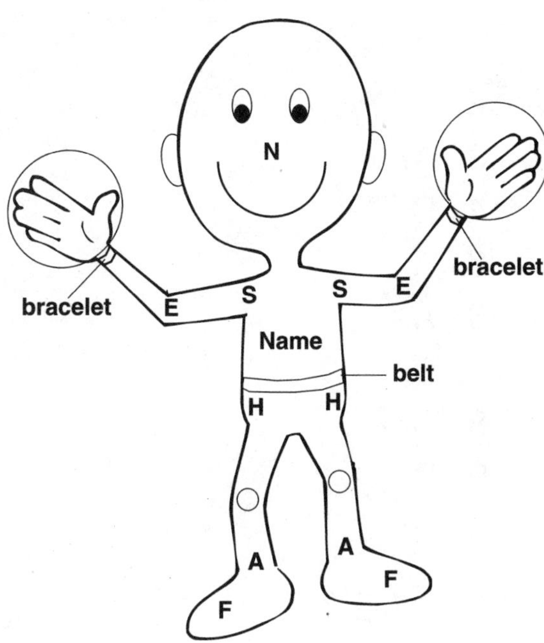


## Bone Zone, pages 32-33

G = green R = red
Y = yellow B = blue

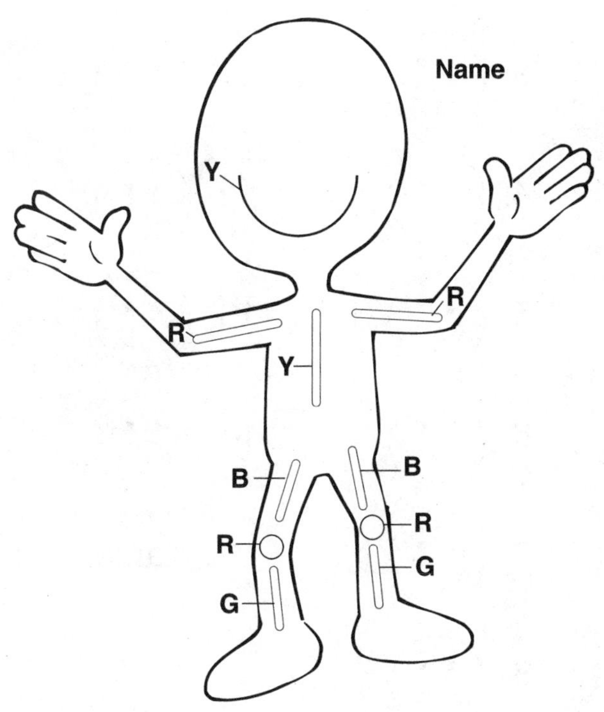


Back:

1. L
2. L
3. P
4. T
5. C
6. A

## Brain Bender, page 34

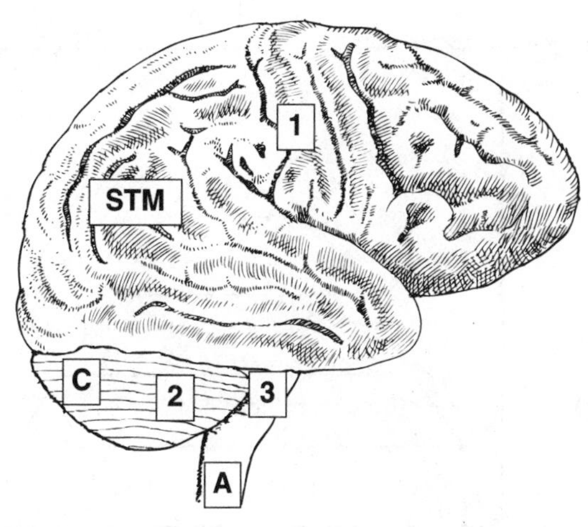


page 35

1. 1
2. 2
3. 1
4. 3
5. 1
6. 3
7. 2
8. 1
9. 3
10. 1

## Pre/Posttest, Part 4, page **37**

Name in top right corner.

1. no
2. yes
3. B.
4. B.
5. frown
6. smile
7. 3
8. dentist
9. Don't play with matches.

### Back

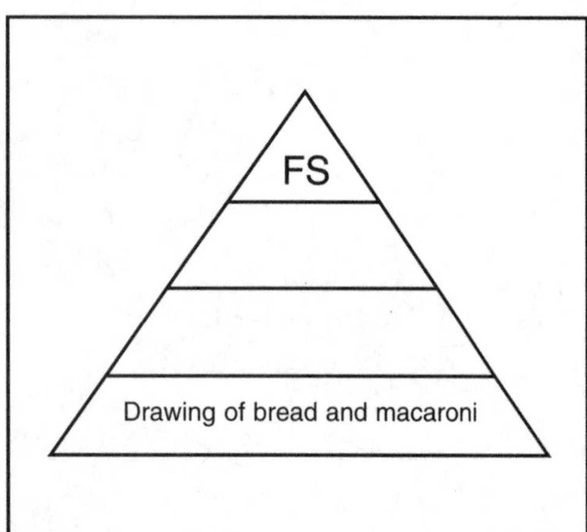


## Thumbs Up, Thumbs Down, page **38**

1. up
2. down
3. down
4. up
5. down
6. up
7. down
8. up
9. down
10. up
11. up
12. down

## Right Choices, page **38**

Name in top left corner.

1. B.
2. A.
3. A.
4. B.
5. A.
6. A.
7. B.
8. B.
9. B.
10. B.

## Smile! page **39**

1. ☺
2. ☹
3. ☹
4. ☺
5. ☺
6. ☹
7. ☺
8. ☹
9. ☹
10. ☺
11. ☹
12. ☹
13. ☺
14. ☹
15. Name

## Careless Carl, pages 40-41

Name at top left. Small box at top right for tally marks. Students should have counted these 12 things (or at least most of them):

1. Carl skipped breakfast.
2. He ran across the street without checking for traffic.
3. Lunch of French fries and cupcakes
4. Darted into the street between parked cars
5. Talked to a stranger
6. Took candy from a stranger
7. Got into a stranger's car
8. Did not fasten seat belts
9. Carl ran into a burning building.
10. Carl dashed under a standing ladder
11. Carl handed the knife with the blade pointed at the worker.
12. Carl drank an unknown liquid.

Drawing of unsafe/unhealthy thing on left and drawing of what Carl should have done on the right. (Drawings will vary.)

## Safety Sort-Out, page 45

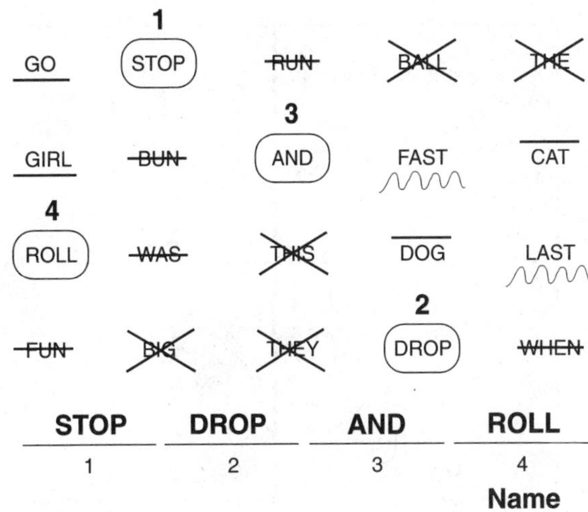


## Pyramid Pointers, page 47

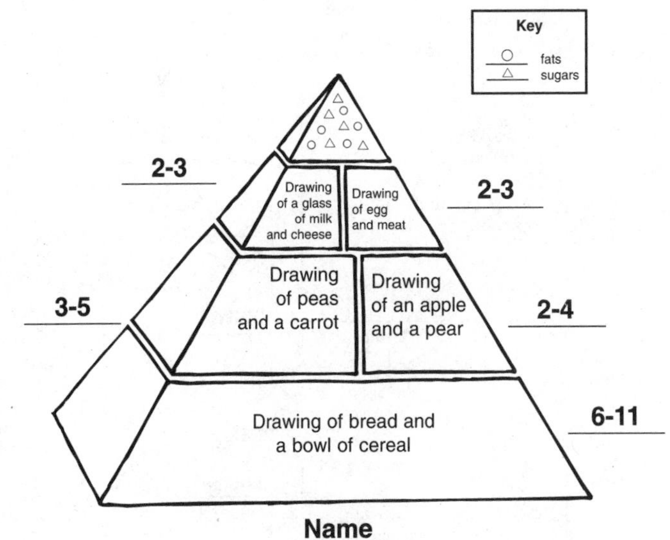

## Vitamins, page 49

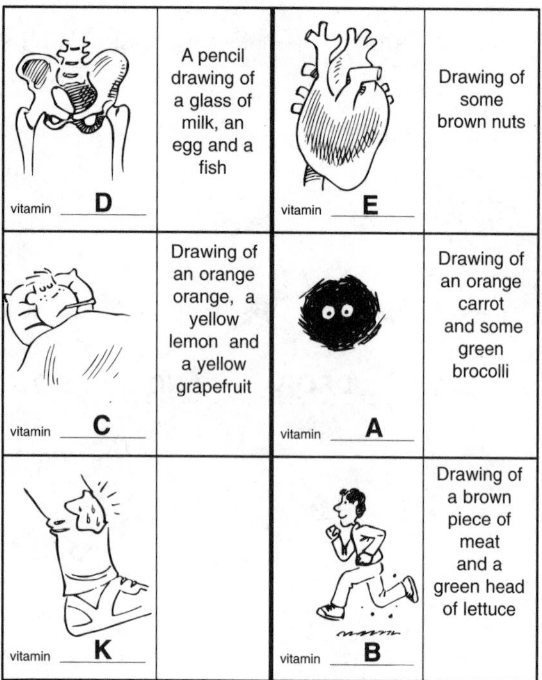


## Pre/Posttest, Part 5, page 51

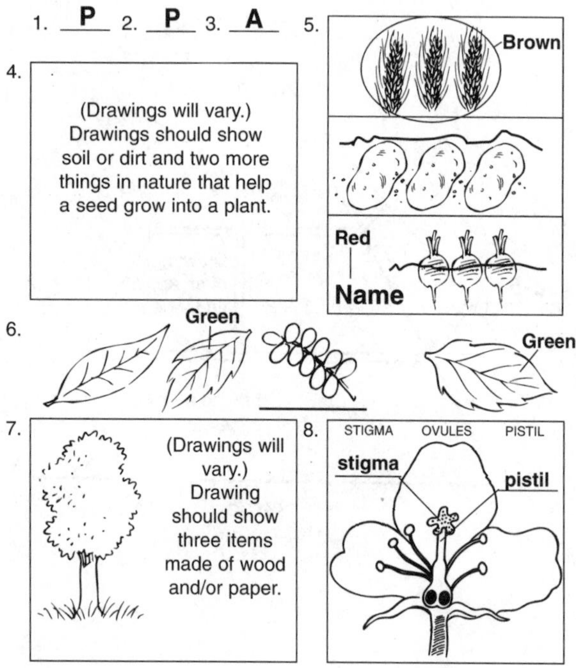


## Plant Food, page 52

1. plant, stand
2. animal, sit
3. plant, stand
4. plant, stand
5. plant, stand
6. animal, sit
7. plant, stand
8. plant, stand
9. animal, sit
10. animal, sit
11. plant, stand
12. animal, sit
13. plant, stand
14. plant, stand
15. animal, sit
16. plant, stand
17. plant, stand
18. plant, stand
19. animal, sit
20. plant, stand

## **Seed Draw,** page **53**

G = green B = brown
Y = yellow

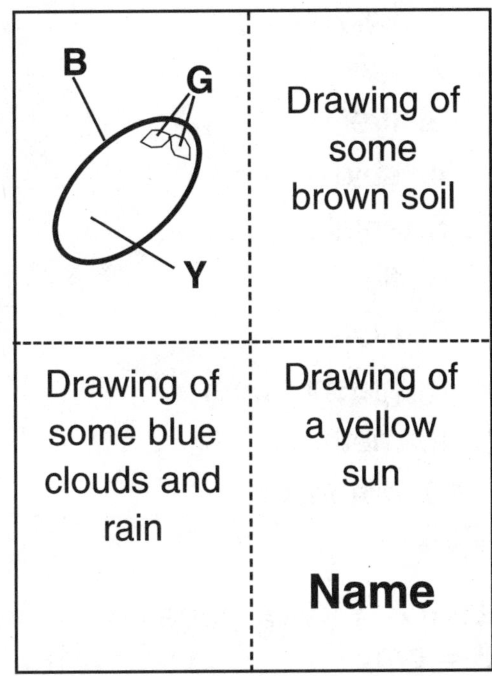


## **Food Riddles,** page **55**

G = green B = brown
Y = yellow O = orange
R = red

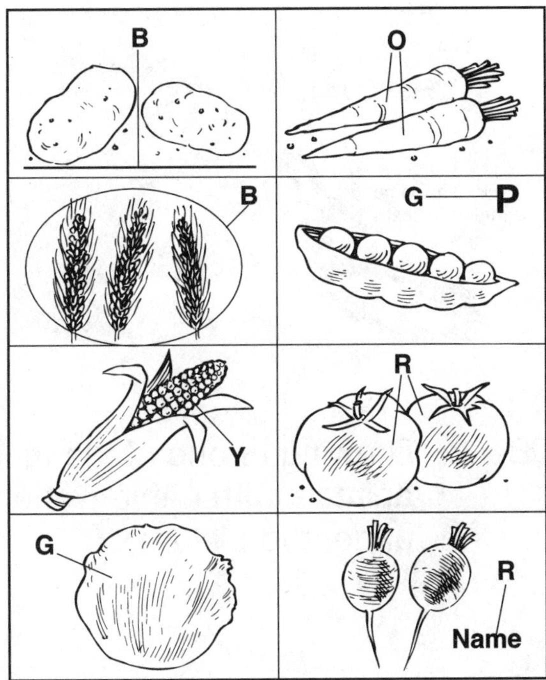


## **Leaf Relief,** page **57**

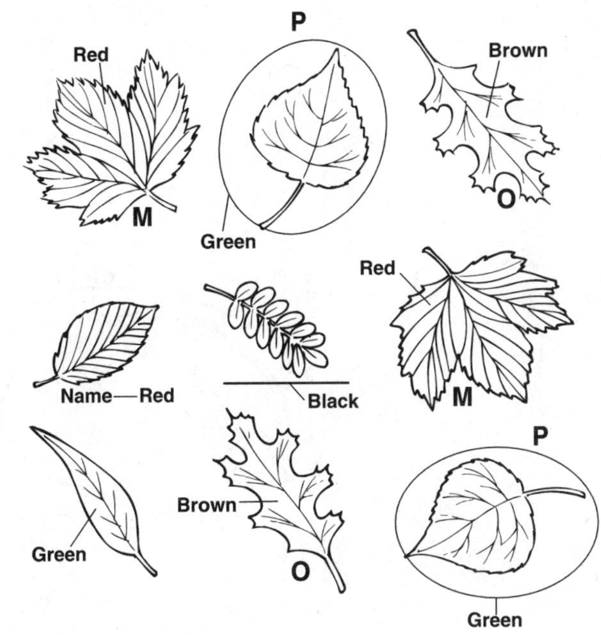


Drawing of a black locust leaf

## **Tree Time,** page **58**

Outcomes will vary. Be sure student has drawn a tree on the left with a trunk, branches and roots. There should be green grass under the trunk of the tree and green leaves on the tree. Name should be written above the tree. In the middle of the paper there should be drawings of three tree fruits. On the right side there should be three products made of wood or paper.

## **Scattered Seeds,** page **59**

Outcomes will vary. The front side of the paper should show two of the six ways seeds are scattered. On the back, there should be one more at the top. The bottom half of the back should contain the student's name and a plant of his choice.

## Flower Parts, page 62

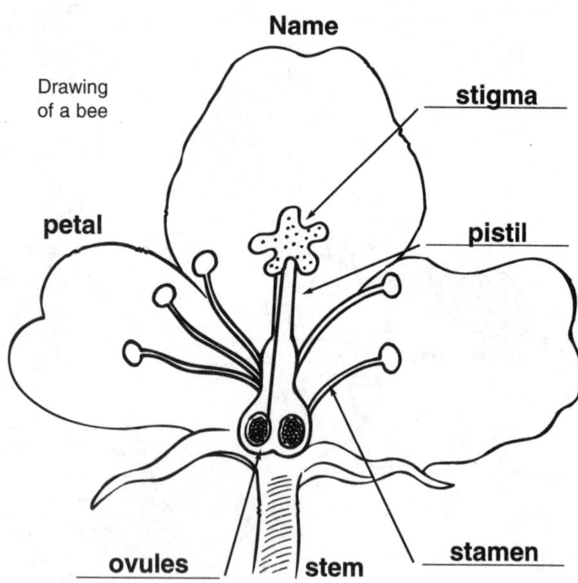


## Pre/Posttest, Part 6, page 64

## Riddles That Will Bug You!

page 65

1. ladybug
2. bee
3. firefly
4. spider
5. snail
6. fly
7. butterfly
8. grasshopper
9. moth
10. dragonfly

## Tundra Time, page 68

G = gray B = brown

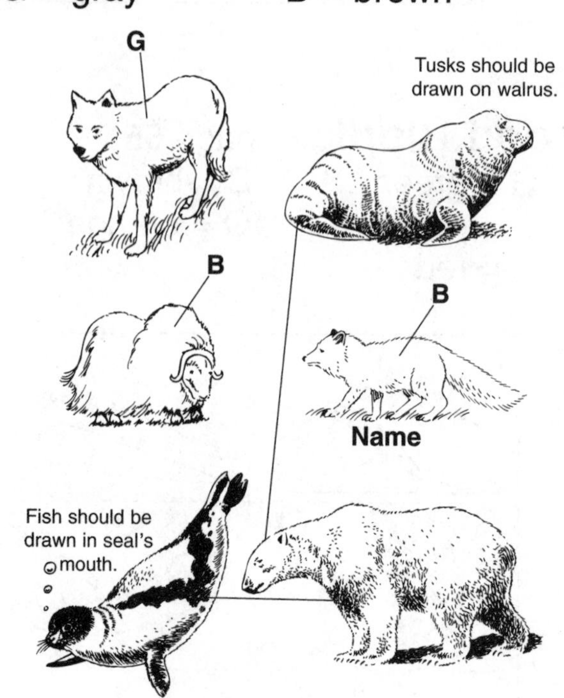


Back: Drawing of one of the tundra animals with name written under the picture.

## Animal Trios, page 69

Name at top of paper.

1. cow
2. pig
3. dog
4. eel
5. fly
6. bat
7. ape
8. bee
9. cat
10. rat
11. owl
12. fox
13. ant
14. yak
15. cub

## Wetlands, page 69

Name at top of paper.

1. L
2. W
3. B
4. W
5. L
6. B
7. W
8. L
9. B
10. B
11. L
12. W
13. B
14. L
15. W

## Mysterious Animals, page 71

G = green R = red
B = blue

Set 1: snake
Set 2: bird
Set 3: sheep

## Dingoes, page 72

Name in top left corner.
Outcomes will vary.

## More About Dingoes, pages 72-73

Name in top right corner.

1. A
2. D
3. W
4. L
5. N
6. 8
7. R
8. B

## Mammals and Reptiles,

page **74**

Name at top of page.

1. M
2. R
3. M
4. M
5. R
6. M
7. M
8. R
9. M
10. R
11. M
12. M
13. R
14. M

## Bird Brains, page 75

1. B.
2. B.
3. A.
4. C.
5. A.
6. C.
7. A.
8. B.
9. B.
10. C.
11. A.
12. B.

Name